Behind the Mind:
Hsin

Translation by Roy Melvyn

Behind the Mind: The Short Discourses of Wu Hsin
Translation by Roy Melvyn
Copyright 2012 Roy Melvyn

Summa Iru Publishing
Boulder. Colorado

Table of Contents

Brief Background

It is widely believed that Wu Hsin was born during the Warring States Period (403-221 BCE), postdating the death of Confucius by more than one hundred years.

This was a period during which the ruling house of Zhou had lost much of its authority and power, and there was increasing violence between states. This situation birthed "the hundred schools", the flourishing of many schools of thought, each setting forth its own concepts of the prerequisites for a return to a state of harmony. The two most influential schools were that of Confucius and the followers of Mozi ("Master Mo"), the Mohists. The latter were critical of the elitist nature and extravagant behaviors of the traditional culture. The philosophical movement associated with the Daodejing also was emerging at this time. Wu Hsin's style of Daoist philosophy developed within the context defined by these three schools and appears to be most heavily influenced by that latter. In addition, it most clearly contains the seeds of what would become Ch'an Buddhism in China or Zen in Japan.

Wu Hsin was born in a village called Meng, in the state of Song. The Pu River in which Wu Hsin was said to have fished was in the state of Chen which had become a territory of Chu. We might say that Wu Hsin was situated in the borderlands between Chu and the central plains—the plains centered around the Yellow River which were the home of the Shang and Zhou cultures. Certainly, as one learns more about the culture of Chu, one senses deep resonances with the aesthetic sensibility of the Daoists, and with Wu Hsin's style in particular.

If the traditional dating is reliable, Wu Hsin would have been a contemporary of Mencius, but one is hard pressed to find any evidence that there was any communication between them. The philosopher Gao Ming, although not a Daoist, was a close friend and stories abound of their philosophical rivalries.

Wu Hsin's work was significant for Daoist religious practitioners who often took ideas and themes from it for their meditation practice, as an example, Sima Chengzhen's 'Treatise on Sitting and Forgetting' (ca. 660 C.E.).

He offers a highly refined view of life and living. When he writes "Nothing appears as it seems", he challenges the reader to question and verify every belief and every assumption.

Brevity was the trademark of his writing style. Whereas his contemporaries were writing lengthy tomes, Wu Hsin's style reflected his sense that words, too, were impediments to the attainment of Understanding; that they were only pointers and nothing more. He would use many of the same words over and over because he felt that people needed to hear words repeatedly, until the Understanding was louder than the words.

His writings are filled with paradoxes, which cause the mind to slow down and, at times, to even stop. Reading Wu Hsin, one must ponder. However, it is not an active pondering, but a passive one, much in the same way as one puts something in the oven and lets it bake for a while.

He repeatedly returns to three key points. First, on the phenomenal plane, when one ceases to resist What-Is and becomes more in harmony with It, one attains a state of Ming, or clear seeing. Having arrived at this point, all action becomes wei wu wei, or action without action (non-forcing) and there is a working in harmony with What-Is to accomplish what is required.

Second, as the clear seeing deepens (what he refers to as the opening of the great gate), the understanding arises that there is no one doing anything and that there is only the One doing everything through the many and diverse objective phenomena which serve as Its instruments.

From this flows the third and last: the seemingly separate me is a misapprehension, created by the mind which divides everything into pseudo-subject (me) and object (the world outside of this me). This seeming two-ness (dva in Sanskrit, duo in Latin, dual in English), this feeling of being separate and apart, is the root cause of unhappiness.

The return to wholeness is nothing more than the end of this division. It is an apperception of the unity between the noumenal and the phenomenal in much the same way as there is a single unity between the sun and sunlight. Then, the pseudo-subject is finally seen as only another object while the true Subjectivity exists prior to the arising of both and is their source.

Translator's Notes

As was customary of the time, a teacher's discourses were usually transcribed by a disciple. The assignment of this task was rotated among disciples on a one-or-more lunar cycle basis without any consideration of the merit of the disciple. It may have been that the task was assigned to whomever Wu Hsin felt needed it the most. That is my speculation only.

When I compare the content of the transcriptions to Wu Hsin's concepts presented in The Lost Writings, they appear to be quite consistent.

Material of this nature is not served well by language. It may seem that there are anomalies and contradictions. So, it is important to state that the translation of Wu Hsin's words herein is not purely literal. Instead, it contains an interpretation of what was clearly implied, and this is where the limitation of words is quite evident.

Compounding this problem, I have chosen to incorporate certain words into the translation which may appear to be incongruent relative to the time of Wu Hsin's writing.

The clearest example of this would be my use of the word ego which wasn't to come into being for many of hundreds of years after Wu Hsin's death.

I have done this to best capture the real essence of the intention behind the word. The original Chinese word 个人 (ge ren) means the individual. However, using the individual doesn't capture the sense of separateness that is better conveyed by ego.

The Sanskrit language also provides us with some marvelous insight. In it, the word for mind is manas, which translated literally means that which measures and compares. That says it pretty well. The Sanskrit word for ego is ahamkara; its translation is I am the doer. Within the context of Wu Hsin's message, the conveyance of the idea of I am the doer is vitally important. As such, this and other small liberties that I have taken with the translation feel more than reasonable.

These pages should not be read with haste; a page or two at a time is sufficient to allow for the content to sink in, as a thrown stone falls to the bottom of the lake.

RM

"Don't ask Wu Hsin to enter into your imagination."

"The world is not in need of improvement.

Stated another way, the world is not the problem. All that's needed is to correct the perspective; not to manipulate, nor to prevent perceptions, thoughts or feelings, nor to avoid what is perceived or thought or felt in the world.

When we stand detached from thinking mind, perceiving senses, doing body, happy/unhappy person, we gain right view.

In that, all is well."

"You have been trained since infancy to direct your attention to what is temporary. Had anyone before revealed the Permanent to you, there would be no need to sit with Wu Hsin.

Most people don't sit because they are afraid of what is revealed. The individuals fear that they will lose their individuality, their identity. One could say that the love of Being is not yet greater than the love of being somebody............... or it could be said that the fear of the not yet known is far greater than the distaste for the known.

Either way, "I'll pay any price" is suddenly shown to be a hollow offer."

"When you become clear that you are not this body, but that it is your instrument, then worries about death dissolve.

In essence, death dies."

The Short Discourses, Part One

The Master entered the Great Hall and began the season's discourses with these words:

Wu Hsin has not visited the abode of truth. Its address is unknown even to him.

Therefore, the focus here is neither on seeking nor finding the truth. Rather, it is weeding out the lies. The discovery of truth is in the discernment of the false.

Wu Hsin is helpless before you in that he cannot transform you into what you already are. In this sense, Wu Hsin bestows the greatest gift to you by informing you that you are not what you seem to be.

This is nothing new; instead, it is the most ancient, transmitted through the silence. Silence is the most powerful instruction. It is the global solvent in which all doubts and questions dissolve. It is the silence that is eloquent.

Wu Hsin's speaking is an interruption to the silence. The silence speaks far louder than any of his words

As such, most of our time together is spent in this silence. For those not yet able to discern from the silence, Wu Hsin will offer a few words daily.

However, be forewarned. Words consistently fail to express the ineffable. Every word approaches it and is then repelled back. More words fail further. Words produce concepts; many words produce many concepts.

In that regard, Wu Hsin speaks minimally, making a point and leaving it up to the listener to allow the words to bask in silence and, in so doing, discern the deeper meaning.

Don't attempt to understand. Don't deal with my words with the intellect; do not commit them to memory. Let the words pass through you, piercing through the mind and through the intellect and returning to their true source.

Wu Hsin is not speaking person to person. Personage is not welcome in this hall. There is no transmission, there is no transmitter, and there is no receiver. You came here as an individual. If you leave as an individual, then you have gotten nothing.

There is some thing which truly is no thing from which every thing is its expression.

I am I, formless, yet appearing as me, with form.

The body, its sensing systems, and the mind are all referenced via "I", that is, I act, I see, I think. These are Its agent, Its instrument.

It is That which exists in and of itself, dependent on nothing, requiring nothing.

It manifests as polarity.

It is Noumenon and phenomena, the One and the Many, the eternal, unchanging, unconditioned juxtaposed with the time bound, changeful, conditioned.

This is the framework which we will develop beginning tomorrow.

With that, he rose and left the Hall.

Today, the Master began:

Most peoples' troubles are symptomatic of a deficiency disease, in this case, the lack of attention. Begin to pay attention and the troubles will go.

The malady is the wrong identification with body, senses and mind, by which we appear bound and therefore unhappy. The remedy is to take your stand prior to the body, senses and mind, to pay attention to the knowing of them. This Knowing is Being and it is present. You are this Knowing Presence.

The mind distorts the gross and overlooks the subtle. It creates a prism of desire and fear through which you create a picture. Can't you see that the representations it creates must be incomplete and incorrect?

Yet, this is what you accept for truth. You believe you were born into a world. It is not so. Each of us creates a world for himself. You live in it, and complain about it.

Your world is comprised of desires and the fulfillment of desires, of fears and the strategies of avoidance. Can't you see that it's your private world? It is little more than an artifact of mind.

Once you see this madness, you are on the way out of it.

See that you create the space in which the world moves, the time in which it lasts. Come to realize that the world is only sand. You may play with it, you may walk on it, but don't build your house there.

There is no journey, as such. It may not seem so, but we are always back where we started. What we were in essence, and what we will be in essence, is what we are in essence.

Ponder this; more tomorrow.

The Master began:

The world springs into view simultaneously with the seer of the world.

There is no process of creation whereas there may be hypotheses of process.

Dreams appear and disappear in like fashion.

The only distinction between the two is duration.

Recognizing the mind means that there is something apart from the mind that has cognized it before, and now has re-cognized it.

The same applies to the body.

All phenomena are recognized by that priormost principle which cannot be seen.

That is all for today.

The Master began:

As one considers all the animals on this earth, one discerns that none are unhappy or dissatisfied other than humans.

This is so because the human intellect purports to know how things "ought to be".

Many pride themselves on their intellect not realizing that it is this very same intellect that makes it almost impossible to apperceive the true state of things.

This explains why so many who claim to have an "intellectual understanding" of this subject matter remain ensnared by their illusions and delusions.

Intellectual understanding is simply not enough. The flaw of intellect is operating within the distorted view of the world. As such, its output must likewise be distorted.

Intuition, on the other hand, is innate Knowing and is therefore far superior to intellect.

The lesson is that using the intellect to reach Understanding is like hiring a blind housepainter.

Ponder this; more tomorrow.

The Master began:

When the viewpoint shifts from being an object to being the very Subject, how can anything take on importance?

That which is truly spiritual is neither physical nor mental. It is that which cannot be confined to any particularized state, any location or any time.

We come to see that there is only one illusion from which all the other illusions come.

It is this: what we appear to be is a phenomenon.......... bound by time, finite and perceivable; whereas what we have been, are, and shall always be, is the noumenon — timeless, spaceless, nameless, formless.

Noumenon manifests itself through endless numbers of forms which are created and destroyed every moment, and in this spontaneous functioning there is no place at all for the notion of any entity.

In this regard, the world is not populated with countless entities.

The world is One Entity; Its name is I.

Ponder this; more tomorrow.

Master said:

All thinking is imaginary because the person talking to you is imaginary.

There is no self talking to yourself; in fact, there also is no "yourself".

Stay a time in silence.

Do not accept these words; look for yourself for "yourself".

He then rose and left the Hall.

The Master began:

Arranging thoughts in a hierarchy of value, the 'I' thought is the first and all important thought.
Within this structure, every subsequent thought becomes "mine".

Following the "I" thought is the not-I thought, that is, thoughts of others and the world.

As such, not-I or the world, is not independent. It requires "I"; therefore, when "I" is not, the world likewise is not.

When the world, the not-I, is ignored, the mind by its very restlessness is obliged to look elsewhere.

This elsewhere is inward, toward one's essence, "I".

The end of the game lies here: he who eliminates everything that is not-I cannot eliminate the "I" as this "I" must be there to declare it. This "I" stands at the terminus of all paths.

It is inviolate.

To one whose eyes are clouded, "I" is limited to the body and the mind.

To the clear, "I" is all.

This is your contemplation for today; more tomorrow

The Master began:

Entry to the Absolute requires leaving the particular behind.

We disengage or detach. This detachment is not by the person; it is from the person.

All attachment implies fear, the misguided assumption that something must be held on to.

It is only when the death grip is released that true freedom from all fears can be known.

All desiring is due to a misguided sense of insufficiency.

All desires' fulfillments are like a meal of rice; a short time later and you are hungry again.

When you know that you lack nothing, that all there is, is you and yours, desire ceases.

Dismount the pendulum of fear and desire. That ground beneath you is the Source and Support.

Ponder this; more tomorrow.

Master said:

The primary benefit to believing in anything is that it keeps one inert and removes the need to investigate the validity of the belief.

In that regard, believing is like a silk blanket that feels good and provides comfort. Sleeping is far more comfortable than the work required for waking oneself up.

Most seekers of so-called truth gladly settle for improvements to their existing fictions.

True investigation must not be supportive of collective pretenses. What the mob believes need not be right and usually isn't.

The rantings of a crazy man have no power over us because we don't believe them. Likewise, the world only has the power we assign to it.

As long as you hold unverified beliefs, believing yourself to be a body in the world for example, the world will impact you.

Experience supports the notion that the greater the doubt, the greater the ensuing clarity.

When you are no longer embrace your belief as a body, you are untouchable.

When your problems are solved, you are also solved. To accomplish this, cease any and all involvement with your so-called life.

In the absence of involvement, there is no judgment and in the absence of judgment, there cannot be any problems.

Yet, paradoxically, you life continues on; you don't fall apart.

He paused.

The Master resumed:

When we are unwilling to accept life on its terms, when we want things to be different from what they are, when we define ourselves by our preferences, all of these sow the seeds of conflict.

What one is conscious of is "of consciousness" only. That is to say that in order to know itself, consciousness objectifies itself.

Thus duality births experience.

Every thing is consciousness. It is that which underlies and unifies all.

Be this and be still.

He sat for some time quietly.

Then, Master continued:

Before there is, before all beginnings, after all endings, I am.

Neither inside nor outside, when all is gone, I remains.

What I am is what I was before this seeming birth.

Nothing has changed except for the fact that I have put on a suit of clothes called "body".

In this world of duality, all I am is its Functioning, the seeing, the hearing, the perceiving, the knowing, and the doing.

Like the wind, I can be experienced but cannot be seen.

Ponder this; more tomorrow.

Questions Answered

On each day of the full moon, the Great Hall is open to visitors. On this day, numerous questions are put forth to Master Wu Hsin. Virtually all the disciples fill every available space toward the back.

Wu Hsin enters and begins:

The purpose of asking questions is not to create a chain of questions. It is to break the endless chain of questions. Bodily identification fuels the questioning.

A single question by each may be put forth and an answer is provided.

This answer must then be given full consideration.

In this way, the cycle of question-answer-question is ended.

It is an individual answer despite the fact that there is no individual.

Now, let us begin.

Q: Master, I have sought after this Totality everywhere without success. What am I to do?
A: The paradox of this Totality is that It is everywhere, yet It cannot be found. Many there are who come to Wu Hsin asking how to find It.
Is this not humorous, how to find "everywhere"?
What shape has the wind?
Very well, this is Wu Hsin's counsel: One can look for It in the space between two heartbeats, two breaths, two thoughts or two objects.

Q: Master Wu Hsin, how can I obtain peace?
A: If you want space, you remove all the rubbish obstructing the space. If you want peace, you remove all the mental rubbish obstructing the peace.
You have been keeping your attention on states that are temporary; now, turn your attention to the Unchanging.

Q: Master, I am worried that previous acts will send me to hell for all eternity. What can I do?
A: Actions can only be deemed to be yours when you define yourself as a body with a name. The actions are the body's, not yours.
Immortality is available to those whose belief "I am this body" has died.

Q: Master, must I give up all my possessions to be with you?
A: No my son. Merely give up the idea of "mine".

Q: Master, what is the importance of my dreams?
A: In the highest sense, the purpose of dreaming is to exemplify how real dream can seem to be.
It is acknowledged that the entirety of dream, that is the dream world and the experiences therein, are contained in the dreamer which is no different from mind.
Is it at least not possible that the same applies to this waking state?

Q: Despite all my efforts, Master, I have not yet been able to see my true nature. What must I do?

A: One's essence, one's true nature, is not perceivable. All attempts to connect the perceptions with essence perpetuate the delusion. One is satisfied to imagine what one is rather than knowing it. Knowing is everything.

Q: Mine is a similar problem and I have been unable to find the solution.
A: All you have been doing is like washing fire.
The only error is looking for solutions in what appears. A permanent solution cannot be found in the temporary.
To cease being the accomplice of this error, one must be no longer willing to assume that what seems to be is what is in fact. It is only when the intellect is thoroughly confused that clarity can dawn.
Direct the attention towards that which exists always and reality rushes in.

Q: Master, when will I have a breakthrough?
A: The initial breakthrough is knowing that Self-attention is far more important than any action that you have to do, than any word that you have to speak, or than any thought that you have to think.
As one cannot obtain an accurate reflection of themselves in running water, so too what is real cannot be accurately discerned by an active mind.

Q: Master, what is the role of the mind in your teaching?
A: Mind is opaque; you cannot see clearly through it. Being a particular personality restricts the vision. It is like looking through a wormhole in a door.
Clear sight is obtained by abidance behind the mind.

Q: Two weeks before, Master, I had beautiful visions of selflessness, peace and unity, every day for six days. Now they are gone. What can I do to bring them back?
A: Enslaved by circumstances, we don't see that we're controlled by the drive for control. Whatever we want to control is the controller. This cannot be taught.
Understanding it is via direct perception, apperception. It does not proceed from or through the mind.
Q: Master Wu Hsin, I feel that I am changing, improving, closer to my goal. What can I do to give more speed to this?

A: Can you fold the sky?

Do not be homesick for a home you never left.

Abiding in Being Conscious is more than mere intellectual accomplishment. The seeker must dissolve.

What remains is what was there at the outset, prior to the installation of any belief.

Q: Master, although years have passed, this sense of a separate self is still here. Can you give me further advice so that I can end its reign?
A: That which arrives spontaneously, departs spontaneously. The self consciousness, the I-am, appeared without any effort on your part. It goes in similar fashion.

No body, no one, can make it go.

I, me, and mine are all creations of the mind. When one abides behind the mind, the triad loses all meaning.

Q: Master, you say that the world is not real. Yet, it continues to feel quite real. How can I reconcile this disparity?
A: The mind imparts reality to everything without checking. As such, unless one is willing to investigate, everything will be real.

Q: How is what I see different from what you see?
A: Prior to clear seeing, what appears is seen as if looking through a keyhole in a door. With clear sight, the door has opened and the world is revealed as the ocean of the mind appearing to Conscious Seeing.

I see myself as both the source and the substance of all there is. Wherever I go I find myself. Regardless of how far I reach out in time, I am there.

Q: I find that it is difficult to move forward as I am beset by many problems. What would you advise, Master?
A: All problems belong to either your body or your mind. Returning to, and resting at, the source of this "your" eliminates all problems.

Q: My enlightenment remains in the distance Master. My efforts have not brought fruit. What should I do?
A: An imagined entity desires to become an enlightened imagined entity. What's the point? It is like trying to measure space.

Yet, this will continue until such time as the distinction is made between this that I am and that that I appear to be.

Q: My life is filled with too many obligations. This, in turn, causes my practice to suffer. What can I do?
A: If you turn the attention to that which illuminates everything, the obligations will be met and the goal will be achieved.

Q: Master Wu Hsin, thoughts continue to intrude on my meditation. I cannot drive them away.
A: One's natural stance is thought-free. Thought arises, projecting a person in a world. It is all imagination. What one truly is is beyond imagination. In that regard, we discover our true self when we stop imagining.
Let the thoughts come but give them no attention.

Q: How can you suggest that the individual is an illusion? It seems to me to be quite real.
A: All apparent actions are the actions of the life force working through the body. It is the sole actor, our beliefs to the contrary notwithstanding.
Upon waking up in the morning, the 'I' that is conscious becomes the 'me', the person. The memories of the previous day and previous days return. The plans for the future continue as before.
This narrative of a self is a collection of past experiences and encounters that are selectively filtered and reframed to maintain a persistent characterization of who we think we are and more importantly, how we would like to be perceived by others.
The body originated as a fertilized ovum. Before it was infused with consciousness, it was inert, dead. When the consciousness is finished, the body is again dead. The body is inert in the same way that a flag is inert. Only when it is powered by the wind can the flag fly. See what it is that powers the body and take your stand there.

Q: When you say that we are blind to the way we are, what do you mean?
A: Our drives as a species are devoted to satisfying desires of sensuality, acquisition, self-affirmation, and security, while protecting ourselves against death or abandonment.

We are blind to the habitual. That which is habitual does not receive attention. As such, we are unaware of our mechanical nature unless it is brought into attention. This requires us to become conscious of things that we normally aren't conscious of. It is only in seeing it that we can begin to transcend it.

Q: Master, I am struggling. The world imposes so many distractions. I can't seem to focus. What would you advise?
A: Treat the world as if it were your shadow. It is there but in no way impedes you. You imagine otherwise, but it is not the case.

Q: Master, what must I give up and what can I retain?
A: Before initiating any strategy of renunciation, initiate a cessation of acquiring.
Once the acquiring has ceased, the renunciation may begin.
This begins by considering what is truly yours that you can give it up.

Q: I feel that I am no nearer to my goal than I was five years ago. What is my error?
A: The fault may be with your goal. The ultimate goal is goallessness. When that is attained, nothing further is required.

Q: What do you advise when seeking a teacher?
A: It is of lesser imperative to seek a teacher than it is to seek what the teacher sought.

Q: Almost every night, out of the silence, a great fear arises. I cannot name it and I cannot control it. What is it, Master?
A: The fear of impersonal being, of not being any thing in particular, restricts almost all from seeing matters clearly. You are face-to-face with nothingness. It cannot harm you. As such, see the baselessness of the fear and allow it to pass.

Q: Master, I have a problem...................
A: When "I have a problem" is properly seen as "'I' is the problem", the problem dissolves.

Q: What is the purpose of practice?
A: The purpose of practice is to make something more natural.
What is already present is what is natural.

How can one practice to be what one already is? It is like looking for shadows on the sun.

What collection of concepts and directions can ever be adequate to the task of taking one beyond all concepts and directions?

Direct apperception cannot be practiced. It is a spontaneous, acausal event.

Q: Is the world of an enlightened one such as yourself the same as my world?

A: The outer world is nothing but sense perceptions. The inner world is nothing but mental conceptions. Since the functioning of the senses and the mind are personal in quality and output, all worlds are personal.

Q: How can I transcend time?

A: Time ceases when the past and the future don't matter any more. All events are transient. An event becomes an experience only when there is involvement. Involvement with the transient is the antithesis of freedom.

Q: Master, I fear death.

A: Only what is temporary can die. Lose your identification with what is temporary and death cannot touch you.

Q: Master Wu Hsin, you said all worlds are personal. I don't understand. Can you speak more on this?

A: Looking through colored glass colors what is seen. Everything depends on the instrument. In that sense, "my" world and "your" world cannot be the same. Whereas seeing is one, seers are infinite.

Q: Master, how am I to act in the world?

A: The world is mere entertainment. It is the enjoyment of the experience of Being Consciousness. The world is nothing but Consciousness, a series of sensations. It is this Consciousness that creates its instrument, its vehicle, the brain in the body.

Have no preoccupation with "how". You will act as is in accordance with your nature. Of this Wu Hsin is certain.

The Short Discourses, Part Two

Today, the Master began:

Most of you are dissatisfied with the way things are. You believe that there could be something more.

Some are just beginning to search for it. Others have been searching unsuccessfully for months, years, and decades.

Why is this so? Maybe it's because you've been looking in the wrong place.

We believe that we know what we are. Wu Hsin challenges that.

What you believe is mere hearsay, told to you over and over by your parents, peers, teachers and society.

You've never taken the time to look and see for yourselves.

That's what is done here.............. and we do that by removing what we aren't and seeing what remains. It is the same method as the sculptor uses.

Many believe that the sculptor adds shape and texture to the raw material to create the sculpture. That's one way of looking at it.

Wu Hsin prefers to see the sculptor as simply removing from the raw material everything that isn't the sculpture.

What remains is the sculpture.

Ponder this; more tomorrow.

Today, the Master began:

In order to examine anything thoroughly, we must be outside of it.

Begin by standing outside yourselves and take a bit of time to view what's there.

Hearsay is information gathered by one person from another person concerning some event, condition, or thing of which the first person had no direct experience.

If one refuses hearsay, what does that leave as "the known"? Very little, it seems.

I am, you are, and this world is. Start there.

These three can be further reduced to perceiving and the objects of perception. Without adding a conceptual structure, allow this to be the point of departure for this investigation.

I was in deep, dreamless sleep. I was dreaming, I was awake: the "I" is present in all three.

Without calling on hearsay, what is this "I"?

Give this your full consideration for the balance of the day; more tomorrow.

Today, the Master began:

It needs to be acknowledged that there is a dysfunctional relationship with the body. That which you are has become enmeshed with it.

To use the term "your body" means that there is a relationship between an as-yet-to-be-defined you, and the object it possesses, body. They are not one and the same.

Your quill is an instrument for writing; it is not you. This body is an instrument for perception and action; it is not you.

It is only because you believe that you reside inside the body that you refer to a sapling as outside the body. If your viewpoint shifted so that you, too, were outside the body, the sapling would no longer be outside the body because the body is no longer the central reference point.

Ponder this; more tomorrow.

Today, the Master began:

When you perceive yourselves as a part of the universe, you must invariably feel apart from the universe. This calls for a correction in viewpoint.

Every operating assumption that you have is calling out for re-examination. In that process, you will discern where the flaws in your point of view lie.

You begin by creating a "me" which is followed by the world, a series of appearances which we label as "other than me".

Then, you appoint this me to godhead status, making it the arbiter of what is deemed right and wrong, what is good and evil, and how things are "supposed to be".

Through "I", you are the acting. Through "my", you are the owning.

You explain, translate, describe, label, define, and separate whatever you perceive every moment of your lives. In so doing, you create a tunnel reality.

This is grand narrative fiction.

Step aside and see how effortlessly and efficiently life functions. That is all that is required is to see things clearly.

However, this cannot occur as long as the seeing is performed through the crystal of the personal. This crystal is what brings distortion to What-Is.

When "me" goes, every "other than me" goes with it.

This is unitive consciousness, the end of distortion.

You continue to be alive and conscious. However, you are no longer self conscious

Ponder this; more tomorrow.

The Master began:

Wherever the mind may go, consciousness is already there.

Asking you mind to define what is real is like asking a cat to guard a saucer of milk. Knowing your mind helps to avoid your mind deceiving you.

Mind and world rise and set together. One cannot exist in the absence of the other. It can therefore be said that consciousness attending to objects is mind.

Realize that every mode of perception is subjective, that what is seen or heard, touched or smelled, felt or thought, expected or imagined, is a representation in the mind.

This realization frees you from the hold on you that it exerts.

Ponder this; more tomorrow.

Today, the Master began:

The past is not-now.

What is not-now has no existence. A thought about the past is referred to as memory; it is a thought about the non-existent, not-now, appearing now.

Likewise, a thought about the future is a thought about the non-existent appearing now.

You are; this is a constant. Can you access the memory of "I was"?

What can be said about those who spend their time attending to what doesn't exist? Are they not dreamers? The label is unimportant. Recognize imagination as imagination and be done with it.

Ponder this; more tomorrow.

Today, the Master began:

Wherever you go, you carry with you the sense of here and now.

This is what distinguishes any present experience from memory.

It reveals that space and time are in you and not the other way around.

Most people are not acquainted with the sense of their being but only with the knowledge of their doing.

However, Wu Hsin declares that there is an organism but no entity to do anything.

The end of separation is the separating yourself from what you are not.

That state in which you remain at any particular moment is then considered to be the waking state and more real than any other

What Wu Hsin is speaking about is not a state. It is That which knows each state: the absence of phenomena, the observing of phenomena and the interaction with phenomena.

The question that normally arises from this is: "What do I need to do to see this?"

However, such a question reveals a lack of understanding. For that which is always there, there is nothing to do.

Ponder this; more tomorrow.

Today, the Master began:

Weren't you a small baby, some years ago?

Where is the baby now? It is gone forever and it is impossible to bring it back. It, in a sense, died while you continued on to become a child, unaffected by its passing.

The child too is gone and you continued to become a teenager, then a young adult and now a full adult. Each died to give way to the next.

Soon the adult will give way to the aged. All these deaths keep succeeding one another. It is the natural course of the form's journey through the world.

Therefore, why fear this impending death? It is no different from the previous deaths. You have known them but you are not them.

Only the name and form die. That which knows the name and form continues.

Fight with all your strength against the idea that you are describable and death cannot touch you.

Ponder this; more tomorrow.

He began:

People seek what they don't have. If they don't have health, they seek health as if it is the ultimate thing.

If they don't have money, they seek money as if it is the ultimate. If they don't have love, they seek love.

When someone goes by this process of asking for what he does not have, they have initiated an endless cycle.

It seems to be taking you somewhere, but it does not really take you anywhere that really matters. Yet you tell yourself that if you don't seek, if you don't desire, you don't go anywhere.

Whether you seek money, or love or knowledge, it's all desire.

The object of desire just changes the direction of your seeking, but it does not change the process of life. And the essence of life rests in its process, in how you are experiencing it right now.

To experience life in a better way, changing the objects of desire is not going to make much of a difference. It is the way we handle the process which is going to make the difference.

Then, one sees that what was really sought all along was the absence of desire

Ponder this; more tomorrow.

Master Wu Hsin began:

All pleasure and pain is mental.

The real Self transcends the mind and is therefore unaffected by pleasure and pain.

These are in and of the mind alone. The proof of this is that these are experienced only when the mind is functioning and not when the mind is still, as in deep sleep.

To be free from suffering the only means, therefore, is to become aware of one's real Self by the investigation suggested by Wu Hsin.

Considering all the happiness you have ever felt, where is it now?

You say it is gone.

Yet when Wu Hsin asks "Gone to where?", you fall silent.

When all tastes are eliminated from the mouth, what remains is the taste of the mouth. When all thoughts are removed from the mind hungry for more and more thought, what remains is the taste of what is referred to as no-mind

Ponder this; more tomorrow.

Master Wu Hsin began:

The piling on of more concepts, this acquisition of additional knowledge, is not the solution. Adding to the known can never take one beyond the known.

At every moment of your life you know what you need to know. Take it to be sufficient.

True knowledge comes via direct apperception and this cannot be forced. It arrives in its own time

Now, be still.

Master continued:

Careful study teaches us that conscious existence continues even in the absence of mind.

It also reveals that peace is present in any moment when there is no thought.

Let there be no confusion.

The purpose of the investigation Wu Hsin proposes is not to establish some special state of mind. Rather, it is to be freed from all states of mind.

Now, be further still.

Master continued:

Once you have recognized the pure taste of tea, you can always enjoy it with sugar and lemon if you so choose.

Discern that the self consciousness or ego is the operative system of this organism. When attention attaches to it, there is enmeshment, entanglement, identification. Unattached, the attention is free.

It is the epitome of peace and you are That.

Now, be still.

Master continued:

The mind reverts to silence spontaneously after every thought. However, another thought comes so quickly, in a seemingly endless stream, that we miss this subtlety.

The mind is purified when it reverts to this silence.

The purification progresses from multiple thoughts to a single thought to no thought.

Now contemplate.

Master continued:

The problem is that the pull of the world is still quite strong for you.

When you realize that everything is in your mind, and that you are beyond the mind, there is a shift in the locus of attention.

The particular no longer holds sway over you; you are now Self-ward facing, and you rest in Being Awareness.

It becomes clear that I-am and the world-is are experienced simultaneously and the body is the instrument that connects the center, the seeing, with the periphery, the seen.

Wu Hsin will return again tomorrow.

Master began:

Where is the past located? Is it not in the mind?

Doesn't the same apply to the future? We can only find it in speculation, imagination.

As the past and future bookend the present, and both are mind only, is it that unreasonable to conclude that the present is likewise mind-stuff?

Later, more.

Master continued:

Enlightenment is one more concept to add to your collection, yet another idea regarding improving yourself, discovering yourself, or obtaining peace and happiness.

There is no awakening for That which never sleeps.

The knower and the known rise and set together while the Knowing never moves.

This Knowing, the true nature of what one is, resides outside the field of consciousness and cannot be known, as such.

Detach yourself from what you imagine yourself to be, from that which are not, and then see if anything else is required.

Ponder this; more tomorrow.

The Master said:

In order that they can be referenced, forms require names.

Prior to receiving a name and knowing oneself to be the name relating to the form, one did not know oneself. It is not prior to consciousness but it is prior to self-consciousness.

When the body awakens in the morning, the world awakens with it. Perceived by the senses and conceived by the brain, this totality seems real.

But this body in this world is temporal, transitory. It comes, it goes.

That which knows all comings and goings stands outside them.

There is no thing independent of It.

Ponder this; more tomorrow.

The Master said:

This sense of a separate entity is like a set of nested dolls. First "I", then "I am" arises, then "I am such and such".

Everything arises when "I am something" arises.

Yet, in the final analysis, the real world is beyond the reach of the human mind.

We experience it through the prism of our desires and fears which frames it as how it relates to the self.

Who goes to sleep and who wakes up? Or better stated, what goes to sleep and what wakes up?

Every morning when you open your eyes, the body wakes up, not you.

The wakefulness which you are is already there. This Conscious Being is the unity that runs throughout the diversity called world.

This world is a mere projection of the mind and the mind is the projecting instrument of Consciousness.

For today, this will suffice.

The Master said:

As you can't have cloth without thread, there can be no appearances in the absence of consciousness.

An individual is one such appearance, the infinite imagined to be a finite fragment.

Only one who establishes an observation post outside of the structure of the individual can have clear sight.

Failing to do this while hoping for clarity is like trying to draw water from a three meter well with a two meter rope.

Enough for today.

The Master said:

The trap is the human propensity to define oneself.........I am this, I am that.

It is a movement away from peace and contentment. True Knowledge is the rejection of the idea "I am some thing".

Being requires no such definition.

You can't use your mind to solve this problem because your mind is the problem.

When the mind is emptied, no longer craving the next idea or the next thought, where is the problem?

For today, this will suffice.

The Master said:

There is an Intelligence operating in all organisms, even organisms without brains, which manages the organisms' life.

What stronger case can there be than this Something unseen, unknown, is at work, functioning at even the subtlest level?

Understand that what is bound to happen will happen.

Events follow one another in endless sequence.

All is the functioning of consciousness through the instruments of consciousness.

There are no entities although there seem to be.

Ponder and meet tomorrow.

The Master said:

Everything one is conscious of serves to remind that one is Consciousness Itself.

Remind yourself often in a similar fashion; in time, it will become automatic.

That is all you will need for today.

Today, the Master began:

So many people are looking for a way, a means to see more clearly.

When Wu Hsin tells them that the way leads through yourself to before yourself; they shake their heads.

They want to add something to themselves, as if a lack needs to be filled. But, adding tin to gold doesn't make better gold.

What you seek is so near you, that there really is no room for a way. Most insist that isn't enough.

So Wu Hsin says that if there is any way, if there is anything that needs to be done, it may very well be simply to listen to the words.

What else is there to do? It is like eating. All you can do is to place the food in your mouth, chew and swallow. Everything that ensues is spontaneous, unconscious and automatic.

Listen only, not with the intellect, but with undistracted listening.

If you use the intellect, you'll end up saying "I understand intellectually, but.............". You may think you have accomplished something, gotten somewhere. But it's not so.

If you listen completely and allow the words to sink down deeply, what needs clarification receives clarification.

Ponder this; more tomorrow.

Today, the Master began:

Man's search for happiness arises out of a skewed perception. "I am not happy...........obtaining such and such will make me happy". It's sort of trying to fill in assumed holes in oneself.

But it is misguided.

If happiness were intrinsic in an object, where in the object is it located? If it is intrinsic, it must always be giving you happiness, from the date of its acquisition until your death. But that is not your experience. The object seemingly provides happiness, but only for a time.

What gave you happiness as a baby does not give you happiness when you became a child. Likewise, as you continue to get older. Each time, some other object takes its place.

As such, happiness is not intrinsic in the objects.

A happiness that comes, will go. Only the happiness that is immanent will never leave.

The happiness you can imagine is far too limited; why settle for a few coins?

So instead of searching for what you do not have, find out what is it that you have never lost?

Ponder this; more tomorrow.

Today, the Master began:

Everything contributes to everything else. No effect has a single cause. Trying to assign causes to events is nothing more than entertainment for the mind.

Assume that Y causes Z. If X causes Y, then is X not also a cause of Z? Can you see how the regression is endless?

When one considers all the conditions that must be satisfied for a single action to occur, the notion of a single cause is revealed as flawed.

If you concede that everything is connected, then it becomes obvious that everything has numerous causes. Yet, if everything causes everything, the notion of cause seems without point.

We only believe we understand causes, but it's self-deception. We conclude that the leaves falling from the trees are the cause of winter, that lightning causes thunder .... and we're self satisfied.

The interconnectedness of everything is such that discerning a single cause for an event is impossible.

We tell ourselves we understand and it is this very misunderstanding that keeps us ensnared.

Ponder this; more tomorrow.

Today, the Master began:

You are constantly striving to be something you are not, because you are afraid of being nothing in particular. Our identity is attached to our "thing-ness".

You live in confusion. It must be this way because you are not reacting to the world as it is. You are reacting to how it appears, as it has been filtered, interpreted and judged by the mind.

The desire for realization is just another escape route. One may say it is a higher escape route, but it is escape nonetheless. It is the dissatisfaction with, refusal to accept, what-is.

Paradoxically, it is the acceptance of what-is that foretells realization.

The end of confusion begins with no longer believing the mind.

Look at things as they truly are. See the mind and the body as reflective of the nature of the organism.

Observe them without judgment. Once they are fully understood, one can move beyond them.

Ponder this; more tomorrow.

Today, the Master began:

Listen to Wu Hsin, but do not expect to benefit in any way.

Who is there to be benefitted?

Any seeming benefit is only another stitch in the tapestry of the personal narrative.

The herbal medicine you require is already growing in your own garden.

You need only look there.

Give that your consideration.

Let us now return to the silence for a time.

Master Wu Hsin continued:

Wu Hsin does not possess even a single concept that can approach the Ultimate.

There are no snares Wu Hsin can set to capture it.

Yet, the fruitless speech continues to issue forth.

Can you now understand why Wu Hsin has nothing to give to you?

Let us pause.

Master Wu Hsin continued:

One cannot apperceive the truth by filtering it through one's concepts of the truth.

Wu Hsin provides the evidence of truth by shining his lamp on untruth.

Wu Hsin never prescribes; he merely describes. Never confuse the descriptions for prescriptions.

Nor does he necessarily provide what is desired, as if a cobbler preparing a pair of sandals to your specifications.

Wu Hsin speaks only of what is, rejecting what is not.

Hearing these words should be like the eating of food: take them in, digest them, extract that which nourishes you and eliminate the rest.

Ponder this; more tomorrow.

The Master began:

All your life, you have known yourself through the body and the mind, through phenomena. Looking at phenomena for knowledge and understanding has become habitual.

How then, can you come to know your true self when it cannot be perceived?

Both the mind and the body are discontinuous. During a single day, they come and they go. Yet, there must be something that is continuous to register the discontinuity.

What you are searching for is not objective. How do you propose to find it?

Can a shadow merge into its source? Can an object know its subject?

Such notions arise from a fragmented point of view.

If one deeply understands that consciousness precedes all appearances and you are that consciousness, that is sufficient.

If anything else is required, it will come in its own time and by its own way.

Ponder this; more tomorrow.

Master began:

Sentience has arisen in an insentient, inert form.

The seeming person is not the perceptual center; the person is one of the many phenomena that the Conscious Life Energy perceives.

Where you are is the site where everything takes place, where all phenomena rise and set.

What you are is the Knowing of the rising and setting.

This is sufficient for today.

The Master began:

I am the point of origin and the terminus. I am Infinite Potentiality, prior to any beginning.

I am that from which all phenomena emerge and return. Unperceivable, I am the Knowing of the presence of all phenomena and the Knowing of their absence.

Because I am, all is; the sun shines, the grass grows and the heart beats. To say more is to be redundant.

As Wu Hsin, I am an expression of this Potentiality at a specific locus of space and time and as Wu Hsin I am Its Instrument of perception and action.

As Wu Hsin, I am a part of a world yet not apart from it.

You are, and you know you are. This is Knowing Presence, your true nature.

To know it is to be It and to be It one must spend time with It. Yet, all your time is spent away from It, entranced by phenomena. As such how can you hope to know It?

Ponder this; more tomorrow.

The Master began:

It's important to understand that there is nothing external which is not first internal.

That Most Internal requires a psychosomatic structure in order to experience Its expressions. All is an appearance in It, perceived and cognized by It.

What you refer to as your world is unique and totally exclusive to you. No one can know what your world and your experiences of it are like, not even Wu Hsin.

So you see, your beliefs shape your experiences which, in turn, reinforce your beliefs. If this dynamic is not broken, you are forever ensnared.

That's why it always comes back to a ruthless examination of one's beliefs.

Ponder this; more tomorrow.

Today, the Master began:

There is endless a cycling from Knowing without an Object to knowledge of an object.

It is in this regard, life appears on Me, to Me.

The individual, although on one level completely illusion, on another level could be said to be particularized consciousness.

When the scope of one's individuality is expanded and expanded, the particular becomes the totality.

Let us now return to the silence for a time.

Master Wu Hsin continued:

The destruction of the world does not affect the space that holds it. With or without this world, the space continues.

When the silversmith melts his coins, how is the silver affected?

In the same way, the death of any individual does not affect the Absolute that ultimately birthed it.

What is real and what is momentary?

In clarifying this, all is clarified.

Let us now return to the silence for a time.

Master Wu Hsin continued:

You are nothing perceivable. You are the perceiving of all that arises.

All experience is of consciousness experiencing itself. If you abide in consciousness everything will be happening spontaneously.

If you are still at the body-with-a-mind level, you will think that you are doing something.

Individuality is a personal matter. When the pure mind or actual-I extends itself beyond the function of observing, a reflected-I arises which one refers to as "me".

To these, Wu Hsin has no attraction. His interest is only in the impersonal.

Ask yourself: stripped of body, senses and mind, what am I?

Ponder this; more tomorrow.

Today, the Master began:

We believe our thoughts because there is an assumption that they state something valid about me, my identity, my happiness or my reality.

There is no evidence that you are a thinker of thoughts. There is no evidence that you are thoughts' creator.

We can say that thought is witnessed or observed. This is not arguable, but it's as far as we can go.

Thoughts come and go in a continuous stream; each departs to make room for the next. The series creates the sense of thinking and we ascribe thinking to mind.

Mind is a process that arises subsequent to your true nature, Knowing. This Knowing cannot be perceived, yet is vividly present and beyond doubt.

We cannot control either the content or the frequency of our thoughts. Why, then, work with thought? What we can do, instead, is to understand the types of thought.

The first kind is of the present moment. It relates to what occupies you right now: solving a puzzle, playing a game, or cleaning a pan. They point to what-is.

All other thoughts relate, in some degree, to what doesn't exist: the past, the future, all imaginations.

Give your attention to the former, ignore the latter and clarity cannot but flood in.

Ponder this; more tomorrow.

Today, the Master began:

All states of mind are just that: states. They come and they go on a background that, for most, remains unexplored.

In this regard, the content of the dreaming and waking states are the add-ons to this background.

Seeing this, one realizes that one is neither the processes of the body nor the brain.

This is the irreversible removal of obstacles to the recognition of that which is eternal and immanent.

It is abidance as the subject, allowing the objects to go in whatever direction they are moved to go.

It is the resolution of the tension between the ongoing sense of self in ordinary experience and the failure to find that self upon rigorous investigation.

Ponder this; more tomorrow.

The Master began:

The brain-in-a-body is the bridge between Consciousness as Subject and Consciousness as Object, that is, manifestation.

 It is the instrument Knowing uses to know Itself. In this sense, consciousness equals experiencing. Experience is the "taste" of consciousness in the same way that sour is the taste of lemon.

Nowhere in the process does there arise the need for a person.

We take a pattern and give it a name. But there's no reality to it. It's merely another thought form, another label.

There is no entity, as such. It is nothing except a set of neurological processes, conceptions and perceptions, and the organism's reactions to these.

What, then, is enlightenment or self realization?

It is an event, the cessation of identification with the limited.

It is a return to that time of the organism before the arising of self consciousness. It is that time before the birth of personhood. As such, no person gets enlightened.

Then, you may well ask, what is a person to do?

You live without self concern. You simply open the door, sit quietly, and see what arrives.

Ponder this; more tomorrow.

The Master began:

Awareness is primordial; it is the original state of Pure Potentiality.
It is beginningless and endless.
Consciousness requires contact with some thing. Essentially, this is
the arising of duality.

The actualization of the Potential yields Consciousness.

There can be no consciousness without awareness as its support, in
much the same ways as silver is the basis for all silver jewelry. And
it is so intimately ours!

When the names and forms are removed, the silver becomes
obvious.

Ponder this; more tomorrow.

Today, the Master began:

Phenomena eclipse the Background. Free yourself from the preoccupation with names and forms and see what remains.

All phenomena point to your existence as the center of perception.

However, until you take your attention off of the pointers, you will remain ensnared.

The senses, by their very nature, chase after pleasant sensations.

That explains why we want to hear great music, see beautiful sights, eat delicious foods, etc.

Yet, this enjoyment is the snare; it binds us to the sensate world. Involvement of any type binds.

Ponder this; more tomorrow.

Today, the Master began:

Setting aside everything we think we know allows wisdom to dawn in us.

What is undeniably observable is that there is a cycling through three distinct states every day. The first two are recurring appearances and non-recurring appearances; they are products of the mind. The third is a blank or the absence of appearances.

Admittedly, there are terms more commonly used for each of these. But Wu Hsin will not refer to them here.

What is telling is simply this: There must be something present in which, on which, and to which the recurring appearances, the non-recurring appearances and the blank arise.

This Knowing of both the particular and the absence of the particular is what one is. To say it another way, it is the knowing of the manifest by the unmanifest.

It is never not here.

Let us now return to the silence for a time.

Master Wu Hsin continued:

Today, Wu Hsin will make an admittedly futile attempt to describe the ineffable:

Amongst the multitude of "thou's" there is a singular I which serves as both their source and destination.

It is the One Principle with different expressions via different instruments.

It is without form and therefore is unaffected by the world of forms.

It is the unification of That which is realized with that which realizes, clarifying the personal aspect of the impersonal.

Once found, it is the satisfaction of the desire to see the seer of seeing, to experience the reasonless joy of the imperishable.

Ponder this; more tomorrow.

Today, the Master began:

Wu Hsin has no interest whether or not his words are compatible
with your beliefs.

When you see yourself as an object in a world of objects, completely
separate from this world outside of you, understand that you are
dreaming. It is mere imagination, confusion between stability and
instability.

To be preoccupied with what you are not is a process without end.
When you speak of "myself", you must clarify what is this "self" and
to what does the "my" apply?

Knowledge of the objective may be vast, but none of it leads to
knowledge of the Subject.

The journey from self consciousness to Consciousness itself is a
reversion of the natural movement toward the object, toward other,
and it shifts the direction toward the subject, toward the Knowing.

In that sense, the first thought has no existence in the absence of
That which knows it. Further, the sense of being, prior to thought, is
the primordial experience.

Ponder this; more tomorrow.

Today, the Master began:

The nature of Consciousness is 'experience' itself.

It is the experience of the absence of content, as in deep sleep.

It is the experience of content as in dream and it is the experience of content and the involvement with said content as in waking.

So, to speak of conscious experience is redundant.

Now, sit in silence.

The Master continued:

"I do not know" offers tremendous possibility.

"I do not know" is the basis of all knowing.

All too often, what passes for the known is merely the believed.

There are an infinite number of ideas and phenomena. All of them are temporary.

As long as the attention is attracted to what is temporary, nothing changes, despite the sense that there is change.

When the attention shifts to the permanent, to the changeless, and stays rooted there, all problems and all questions dissolve.

Let us now return to the silence for a time.

Master Wu Hsin continued:

Wu Hsin declares that there is no going beyond.

There is only returning to before.

Who is to realize what, and how, when all that exists is the Conscious Presence and nothing but the Conscious Presence?

When Wu Hsin arrived, he brought the world with him.

When he departs, it too will go.

At the core, there is consciousness in which everything appears.

Where is the problem unless we are creating stories about the appearances?

Ponder this; more tomorrow.

The Master arrived late today

You are infinite potential and inexhaustible possibility. Because you are, anything can be.

However, you are presently abiding as such and such an individual. Until this is thoroughly seen through, you are like a water buffalo in deep mud.

That is why Wu Hsin's words have a singular purpose, to destroy all belief in the existence of any subjective object.

When you say "I see a mountain", what you are saying is that the eye, which is an objective instrument, in the body, which is another objective instrument, sees the mountain, another object.

There is no subjectivity to be found and, as such, the statement cannot be true.

It would be much more accurate to say "I sees the mountain" wherein this "I" is the Subjectivity Itself

Ponder this; more tomorrow.

Today, the Master began:

There is a single Subject.

You have lost your identity with this Subject that you truly are and have mistakenly identified yourself with an objective "me".

Yet, this "me" is nothing but an idea, a thought. It has no substance other than that which you assign to it.

When the Conscious Life Energy in the male seed finds an egg-host, a new life begins.

However, there is no special "you" in it. The "you" is just a mental construct, a way in which the brain protects the body.

Mind is both the actor and the stage whereon the particular and the universal are inseparable.

There is functioning, the seeing, the hearing, the movements.

But there is no "you seeing'.

Ponder this; more tomorrow.

The Great Hall is full as we await his arrival. Master begins:

Suppose someone is one hundred years of age. It has been one hundred years of becoming; becoming this, becoming that.

But these becomings, these movements from infant to adolescent to adult to old man are changes appearing in the changeless.

Becoming is always of what one is not, it is always a movement away from, a fractionalization of, what one is.

Let us not preoccupy ourselves with becoming. Let us stay here, be here, be.

Let us now return to the silence for a time.

Master Wu Hsin continued:

It is, in a way, perverse that there is so little to really discuss.

All there is, is being and the knowledge of being. This is irrefutable.

The discussion should end here because all else is conceptual and can be argued endlessly.

Yet, we continue talking.

What must be made clear is that the brain is an object. As such, anything resulting from brain activity cannot be subjective.

The subjective, the Single Subject, therefore remains elusive.

Let us now return to the silence for a time.

Master Wu Hsin continued:

One need not make any effort to be, to see, to taste, to smell, etc. All of it occurs spontaneously.

Likewise, that which is seen, tasted, and smelled also arises and sets spontaneously. The day begins spontaneously and ends spontaneously. You don't will yourself to sleep or to awaken.

So, who is doing anything?

Where is the need for various practices in order to become what you already are? See it, then be It.

Ponder this; more tomorrow.

Master Wu Hsin began:

All things personal appear and disappear, perhaps to appear again, perhaps not.

But, when you are nothing in particular, how can you be harmed?

The insanity of it all is that the so-called seekers want to reach this "nothing in particular" while retaining their individuality.

Individuality is the price and there are a rare few willing to pay it.

He then rose and departed the Hall.

Master Wu Hsin began:

We gather here to glean the reality underlying your seeming state.

Light goes out thru the windows from the lamp that is lit inside. We are here to light that lamp.

The peace you say comes and goes is false peace. It's not the real peace because it is subject to conditions.

The only thing that stands in the way between you and unwavering peace are the concepts and beliefs you hold.

Divest yourself of them and Wu Hsin guarantees your peacefulness.

To state it a bit differently, the challenge before you is the conquest of your imagination.

Give your full consideration to this.

Master Wu Hsin began:

Most of life is lived automatically, below the threshold of conscious attention.

The body functions this way too, most effectively.

When you can allow everything to unfold in its own time and in its own way, a relaxation will sweep over you like nothing you have ever known before.

Your wants dissolve, freeing up a huge reservoir of energies that had been previously allocated toward the satisfaction of desires.

It is through this that you come to understand that everything perceivable is transient, and only being, 'I am', endures.

What is "not you" and "not yours" becomes clear and obvious.

Ponder these words; more tomorrow.

Master Wu Hsin began:

Empty your storehouse of concepts and ideas.

Money that is borrowed is not yours.

When you fill a cup in the river, the water is not yours.

In the same way, you've taken endless ideas and concepts from others and now call them your own.

When the storehouse has been emptied, investigate what remains.

Let us now return to the silence for a time.

Master Wu Hsin continued:

Striving for betterment is merely a subtle form of control, to control the quality of the experiences that come.

It is always that which we seek to control that ultimately controls us.

Therefore, in so doing, we merely provide reinforcement to the prison doors.

In other words, you are your only obstacle.

Let us now return to the silence for a time.

Master Wu Hsin continued:

Energy moving through the ocean is called waves. When it moves through the air, you call it wind. When it moves through this body, you call it "you".

Understand that you do not move, only the scenes change. That is to say that there are movements in consciousness while consciousness is unmoving.

The waking, dreaming, and sleeping states pass before you.

Regardless of what appears or disappears, that which cognizes appearance and disappearance is fixed.

Paradoxically, this Most Antecedent Principle cannot be known because for it to be known it would have to be an object of knowledge.

Ponder this; more tomorrow.

Master Wu Hsin began:

You cannot be what belongs to you. If you say "I am my cart", people will think you're mad. So why do you believe that you are your body and you are your mind?

In a similar fashion, you can't be what you are conscious of. You must be prior to it.

Begin with "I am nothing perceivable" and stay with that for some time.

Once there is a deep feeling for it, move on to "I am nothing conceivable" and do the same. The former eliminates the body as "I" and the latter does the same for the mind.

By proving that you are not the body and its senses or the mind, and standing separate from them, you remain in your real Self.

According to this approach, everything, from the intellect down to the body and the world, become objects to be separated from you.

You will come to see that being what one is occurs naturally when one ceases being what one isn't.

When your attention is off a thing and not yet fixed on another, in the interval you are your Self.

In most cases, notions of "me" and "mine" are transformed slowly, impeded by imagination.

It is much like ice which turns to water and water to vapor, and vapor dissolves in air and disappears in space.

Take hold of "I cannot be whatever appears before me."

As such, whatever I perceive, is not what I am. I am the very perceiving itself" and allow it to do its work.

The progression is often from objects of consciousness to objects in consciousness to objects as consciousness.

Ponder this; more tomorrow.

Master Wu Hsin began:

We say that the body is a corpse once dead.

But the truth is that the body is always a corpse insofar as it is inert and requires animation.

Therefore, what is one other than an animation, an event of a fixed duration?

One sincerely sets out to find this "me" but all that is found is a story, a detailed narrative. But there's no substance to it.

I, as the potential source of all experience, experiences the apparent universe through a psychosomatic apparatus. But this is the experience of appearances.

What you truly are is waiting for you behind all experience.

Cease taking yourself to be within the field of consciousness.

That which perceives is not the body, which is only an object since it also can be perceived. The knower and the known are both objects.

It is the Knowing that is the subjective element and needs to be the focal point of attention.

Ponder this; more tomorrow.

Master Wu Hsin began:

One experiences oneself as a body and a mind independently acting in the world.

When one recognizes that the way one experiences oneself is a skewed representation, it becomes easy to accept that the way one experiences the world is likewise a skewed representation.

The Subjective functioning is all that is, the seeing, hearing, feeling, tasting, smelling, thinking, and acting in the objective manifestation via the psychosomatic instrument that is fitted into the manifestation.

Those who succeed in adapting their viewpoint in alignment with this know only peace.

Let us now return to the silence for a time.

Master Wu Hsin continued:

You begin here and you come to learn that there is no "there".

The five senses cannot help one to transcend the world; in fact, they keep one mired in it.

One's captivation and fixated interest in external objects is a misdirection of consciousness itself.

Attention must be moved from phenomena to Noumenon.

It is the source of everything; it is the destination of everything and it is the space between the two.

Ponder this; more tomorrow.

Master Wu Hsin began:

How much must you exert to have a great idea?

Great ideas are not a function of effort; they are spontaneous arisings.

What effort did you make to become self conscious?

It is the same effort required to remove it!

There is no fixed or prescribed method in which the Self reveals Itself.

When you are one with the sense of conscious presence, then whatever is necessary will sprout by itself; that is to say, if the self consciousness is to go, it will go spontaneously.

Ponder this; more tomorrow.

Master Wu Hsin began:

The body is in the mind which is localized in the brain.

This, in turn, functions via the Conscious Life Energy.

Disregard the psychic life you struggle so hard to nurture and maintain.

Stop fixating on the arriving thoughts and see what has been, is, and always will be.

This Constant is what you are.

By comparison, the world, and all its components, is the shadow of the formless.

Ponder this; more tomorrow.

Master Wu Hsin began:

What is to be understood is that you are in essence The Complex which is formed by consciousness and the life force. The world is an afterthought. It doesn't matter.

This Complex provides sentience and activity to the body. It provides beingness and functioning to the world.

Yet, they are merely an appearance; they don't matter. It is like the way things were prior to the arrival of self-consciousness. Nothing was of any value.

They don't matter in the same way that the burning wood has no interest in whether or not the stove heats evenly. Smoke does not disturb the sun. The wind doesn't care about the kite's dance.

As one has no interest in what the neighbor down the street is doing, have no concern for the activities of the body. It does what it does and fulfills its role.

Remaining as The Complex, all is peace. Phenomena appear and disappear; the space remains.

The world doesn't matter.

Think of this today.

Master Wu Hsin began:

Subjectivity is the true state.

Whatever one does to remind oneself of one's subjectivity is a movement in the direction of abidance there.

Therefore, one watches the mind to discern one is not the mind.

Once everything that is known is rejected, what remains is what also has been known, the Conscious Life Energy, but has been ignored.

That is your true state.

Mind is a series of processes in humans. Mind can no more volitionally be stopped than can digestion and elimination. Only that which animates the mind can stop it.

Deep understanding of this will allow you to see clearly that you are an instrument of the Conscious Life Energy. There is not a single thing you can do to contravene its movements.

Once this is seen, you can relax.

Ponder this; more tomorrow.

Master Wu Hsin began:

Religion is a collection of beliefs, unverified certainties and worldviews that are built around narratives, symbols, and histories. It is intended to provide meaning to a personal life.

By far, the religion with the most adherents is the Religion of the Individual. Its main tenets are:

* We are born; we die. In between, is the life we live.
* We are a separate entity in a world of other separate entities.
* The world existed before we came into it and will continue to do so after we depart from it.
* Everything I claim to be mine is in fact so.
* Phenomena exist independent of their perception.
* We are the knowing subject of every object.
* We are the ultimate initiator, the doer, the thinker, the feeler, the choice maker.
* Mind is produced somewhere in the body and is therefore personal.
* Consciousness is epiphenomenal of mind and is likewise personal.

When these tenets are examined rigorously, the Religion of the Individual crumbles and is replaced with the clear sight of What-Is.

Ponder this; more tomorrow.

Master Wu Hsin began:

Whatever occurs in the body and whatever occurs by the body is the action of the Conscious Life Energy. Its sole declaration is "I am". Its father is "I will be".

You say "I am speaking", "I am working". Is it not illusion to believe that the actions occurring via the functioning of the Conscious Life Energy are yours?

Are they anything more than the music that emerges from the instrument?

Make the "I" and the "am" a single word and follow each instance with "is".

We now have I-am is speaking, I-am is working.

This is the true state of affairs.

Let us now return to the silence for a time.

Master Wu Hsin continued:

Consciousness, being time bound, is the actualization of the Dynamic Potentiality.

Understand that manifestation is the spacio-temporal expression of consciousness.

Therefore, there is consciousness prior to manifestation, consciousness of temporal manifestation and consciousness of spacio-temporal manifestation.

These are the 3 states of consciousness.

The last two could be said to comprise a singular state, the state of appearances in consciousness.

The end of the scrutiny on objects in these two is the beginning of the scrutiny on subjectivity.

The conclusion of the scrutiny on first person is the dawning of the true Knowing.

Once dawned, it is seen that that there is no difference between Being and Knowing.

Your work is done.

Ponder this; more tomorrow.

Master Wu Hsin began:

Dissatisfaction with What-Is is a great impediment.

We search in every direction for a remedy to the dissatisfaction.

Only when it is seen clearly that the remedy is directionless, when we allow ourselves to be where we are, we can then know what we are.

Knowing what we are, all dissatisfactions, all questions end and what we are is then their answer.

We are taught that happiness is attained via the Path of Acquiring. The evidence is not supportive of this.

On the other hand, the Path of Relinquishing has proven, time and again, to be an efficient means.

The former enslaves whereas the latter liberates.

In giving up everything, you learn that you need nothing.

Ponder this; more tomorrow.

Master Wu Hsin began:

What is your world?

Is it anything other than a field, well furnished with what you think are flawless memories added to your imaginations, seeming knowledge, and anticipations?

Your world appears and disappears, and is ever-colored by the state of your mind. It is entirely private.

You can't share it with Wu Hsin so that he may partake in your experience of it.

If you can't share it, how can you claim that it is real?

Therefore, it cannot be. It may appear to you, but it has no true being.

Ponder this; more tomorrow.

The Master arrived late to the Hall. It is clear that he is feeling ill.

All problems and questions are based on one's identity with the body and mind as an individual.

If that identification is not there, then neither problems nor questions can arise.

Thus, the intention is to end the feeling of separation from That because of which we know we exist.

There may arise a fear of losing yourself.

However, you can never lose yourself; you can only lose ideas about yourself.

Ponder all this; more tomorrow.

Master Wu Hsin began:

The world of objects and subjects is relatively real. That is to say that it appears real from the inside looking out.

From the outside looking in, it is most clear that the world is a temporal projection, a superimposition.

Abiding outside of the relative is sometimes called realization. It is the realization of the Real.

The point of view is paramount.

Smoke may obscure the sun, yet the sun knows no such obscuration..

Let us now return to the silence for a time.

The Master continued:

Thinking may or may not stop.

However, if you listen to the words of Wu Hsin, any thoughts that appear will no longer be deemed yours.

You can live without thoughts, but thoughts cannot live without your sustaining them.

Don't allow your mind to take you away from the immediacy of Consciousness. This Consciousness is what the mind appears to.

The subtlety here makes it easy to miss, like looking for a black cat in a darkened room.

So you look and then you look again.

Ponder this; more tomorrow.

The Master began:

Consciousness experiences its manifestation via 3 cyclical states; they are commonly referred to as waking, dream and sleep.

Instead, Wu Hsin suggests that they be called the experience of mind and matter, the experience of mind, the experience of nothing to experience.

One could also say that the three are: the appearance and disappearance of mental and physical phenomena, the appearance and disappearance of mental phenomena, the absence of phenomena.

Yet a third alternative would be Consciousness plus time plus space, Consciousness plus time, Consciousness plus relative absence.

In any of these, consciousness stands as the background, the screen on which each comes and goes.

Ponder this; more tomorrow.

The Master began:

Wherever one's mind goes, consciousness is already there.

The mind, by its very nature, is compelled to objectify the sense of I-am. It does so by extending I-am into I am this body, then into I am this body in this world.

"I am this body in the world" is the herald of the mind flow. This is temporary, appearing on a background of permanence.

This sense must be refined via what we call returning until each adjunct is removed, leaving only "I", the true Self, That which serves to support "I am this body in the world".

You begin from where you are, which is awash in thoughts, one following the other in endless succession.

Returning involves going from this condition to a reduction in thoughts, to the holding of a singular thought, to the absence of thought.

Of all the singular thoughts to be held, the sense of being, I or I-am, is the best.

Ponder this; more tomorrow.

The Master began:

Images do not exist by themselves. They only exist as the brain's representations of the incoming data feed, the movements of energy perceived by the sense organs.

No one argues with the notion that imagination is untrue. The challenge set out, then, is to investigate how much time is spent in imagination.

One fully enjoys the world only when one has no vested interest in it.

One must remember that an entry is also an exit. We seemingly enter into the world through I-am and return to prior to the world by exiting through I-am.

The dream lasts as long as the dreamer. The end of the latter is the end of the former. Although it may not seem so, the same can be said for the world and the individual.

The world is very seductive. It creates a force that draws attention toward it.

Unless and until there is a countering pull from Conscious Being Itself, clarity is not possible.

Ponder this; more tomorrow.

The Master began:

Can an appearance discover that it is an appearance?

As long as there is no insight into the appearance being an appearance, what can be done.................. and by whom?

Can you admit that every investigation and any possible proof, take place in the very appearance where the appearance itself is?

What is undeniable is that if the person is an appearance, then the world in which the person lives is also an appearance.

When we examine ourselves deeply, we are able to see more clearly the dimensions of the prison that have built around ourselves.

What is so paradoxical is that we fight hardest for that which we need least.

Ponder this; Wu Hsin will speak more tomorrow.

The Master began:

If You are absent, then no thing is. This You is Conscious Life Energy.

If the bowl of sugar is removed, what is the likelihood that the cup of tea can be made sweet?

In the absence of this Conscious Life Energy, what can exist and who is there to know it?

What occurs is that this Conscious Life Energy localizes as mind.

The mind, in turn, reframes the functioning by reorganizing it around a central reference point, me.

But, this me is only a label: body and its actions, mind and its narratives, ideas and beliefs.

When a thought appears, the mind generates an "I think".

Ponder this; more tomorrow.

The Master began:

There is no method for getting rid of what doesn't exist.

This world is like an intricate spider web. Once entangled in it, it is difficult to get free.

Remembering that not a single thought is accompanied by a certificate of ownership is helpful in this regard.

We live in our own narrow, limited world commanded by associations from all our subjective impressions. This could be called a prison, except for the fact that we voluntarily return to it time and again.

Thoughts are temporary. Things are temporary. All appearances are temporary, appearing on the intemporal.

The world we experience around us is no more "out there" than are our dreams.

That point at which the world suddenly appears is the intersection between duality and the non-dual.

In the body, there is a current of energy and intelligence which guides, maintains and energizes the body. In attending to that, the world loses its importance.

When waking up in the morning happens, it begins with the thought of I-am, and then the entire world appears as I am this and there is that.

Whatever differences may appear make no difference in the functioning of totality. They only impact the seeming "your world".

Let this be your contemplation for today.

The Master began:

A distinction must be drawn between what comes and goes and what does not. The former may be labeled "appearances" and the latter "actuality".

Since the attention can only go to one at any time, each must decide where the attention is placed.

Actions, perceptions, thoughts and feelings all come and go.

But the knowing of each never departs, not even for even the smallest unit of time.

As such, Knowing cannot be an activity, since activity starts and ends. This Eternal Constant, Knowing, is what one is. When one distances oneself from one's image of oneself, this becomes clear.

All satisfaction, seeming derived from objects and experiences, is actually derived from the cessation for the desire for the object.

In the absence of desire, one's natural state of satisfaction and peace shines forth.

Let this be your contemplation for today.

The Master began:

Before attention can be redirected, inattention must be acknowledged.

Belief is the currency of delusion. We do not so much observe what is as we do conjure what appears to be.

Beneath a rock, there is always darkness regardless of how bright the sun shines. To begin to get out from "under", one need not fully understand; one begins by ceasing to misunderstand.

How do we see an object?

The sense organ provides the form while the mind supplies concepts or ideas. But it is only Knowing, the Self, which provides the sense of being. Whatever is observed points back to the perceiving center.

Memory is what makes life appear to be continuous. However, the body, the mind, and the world are really all discontinuous. They are mere appearances on That which is continuous.

Ponder this; more tomorrow.

The Master began:

Most people think they need to have some sort of practice. Stop thinking and then revisit the issue.

No-mind is when mind has nothing to say. In it, everything that comes is welcomed because no preferences are held.

Now-here is the spatio-temporal point at which life and living occur. Any movement away from it is movement into imagination.

Problems are thoughts and thoughts are problems.

Vast leaps in understanding occur when, instead of building onto what is thought to be known, one discards what is thought to be known.

Sensations, thoughts and feelings are all perceptions. What is it that perceives? It is That which never sleeps, which ever-is.

The brain filters all incoming data for relevance. It then allocates what it deems relevant to memory and rejects the rest.

The brain imparts its reality to everything that passes through it. However, the brain's reality is not reality. It is a representation, albeit an inaccurate one.

Things are as they are, because we accept them as they are. When we stop accepting them and begin to investigate, they will dissolve.

Ponder this; more tomorrow.

The Master began:

The mind is so small that it can only hold one thought at a time. As such, there is no difference between mind and thought.

There is no dreaming in dreaming. There is only dreaming upon reflection when waking.

A dream is only labeled a dream when it is in the past. At the moment of experiencing both the dream state and the waking state, no differences between the two can be discerned. Both are taken to be real as they occur.

Thinking of what cannot be thought is still a form of thought. One cannot conceive of what lies beyond the mind. One must go there.

Thoughts enslave when their ownership is claimed. When the thoughts are not yours, they cannot exert any power over you.

To see oneself as one is would be to perceive what is real, a direct perception that is possible only in a state free of all conditioning. In the conditioned existence, what is perceived is filtered and can therefore be said to be a fabrication.

Let this be your contemplation for today.

The Master began:

We are most eager to believe and far less eager to know.

We cannot fully understand something while being involved with it. It is only when we move out of it that we can begin to see clearly. With our heads in the clouds, we can't see outside the clouds.

When it is seen that everything outside is experienced inside, ideas of inside and outside lose their meaning.

When one is wholly identified with the body and mind, one is completely absent from one's essential nature. How can anyone awaken until they see that they are asleep?

When the attention is moved from there, that being the world, to here, that being Conscious Existence, not a single problem can be found.

Let this be your contemplation for today.

The Master began:

With the arrival of clear sight, only the reflections change, only the false dies. What is true, what is real, is eternal.

There seems to be a seer and an object. But upon direct investigation, nobody experiences a seer, only seeing.

Thought impedes the flow of reality.

Realizing that the thinker is just another thought obliterates the concept.

With regard to the perception of any object, the senses provide the form whereas the mind supplies the labels and concepts. Yet, there are no objects without the subject, no phenomena in the absence of noumenon. As such, for anything to be, Consciousness has to be there first.

Whatever is known is in the field of consciousness and is therefore known by consciousness. It is the actualization of infinite Potentiality.

The ideas of exterior and interior, of inner and outer, exist only so long as you do not accept an absence of separation.

Let this be your contemplation for today.

The Master began:

I cannot speak of the mind's natural state. The mind's natural state is thoughtlessness. No thought, no mind.

In clarity, one's mind becomes like the moon at noon.

Only imperfect knowledge requires a load of words.Reality is everywhere except inside one's head.

Reject all second hand knowledge, all hearsay, all the knowledge that has been acquired.

Begin with the only firsthand knowledge one has: I am and I know that I am. Don't add anything to it, stay with it and see where it takes you.

Those seeking clarity are well advised to remember: "You can't take you with you".

Those who are asleep rest in what is known while those who are awake bask in the unknown.

Those who have apperceived their immortality no longer worry about death. It would be like worrying about falling off the floor.

Let this be your contemplation for today.

The Master began:

True happiness is unassailable because it is not conditioned upon this or that.

When I-am is attached to anything creating "I am this" or "I am that", another delusion is formed.

With clear sight, the world doesn't matter.

The only impediment to lasting happiness is unhappiness.
Unhappiness is nothing more than the thought "I am unhappy".
When the thought goes, unhappiness goes.

All thought begins rooted in memory, in the already-known, the past. In it, everything is defined, labeled, and filed away. In this manner, re-cognition is facilitated.

Let us now return to the silence for a time.

The Master continued:

Soul, mind or ego are words only. There are no entities that they correspond to.

Spirituality with the intention of improving the individual in any way is not spiritual.

"I-am-this" is the Primary Thought, the central reference point around which all perspectives evolve.

The challenges may be new, but the responses are too often old, having been accessed from memory.

The ego comes and goes; that which observes its coming and going is what one truly is.

Let us now return to the silence for a time.

The Master continued:

The so called witness that is enmeshed in what he perceives is merely the ego in disguise.

The witness who is unmoved and untouched, is the guardian of the real, the contact point between the unmanifest and the manifested.

There is no individual consciousness because there is no individual.

There must be something to say "There is nothing".

This arrival of self-consciousness is the source of all dissatisfaction, unhappiness, etc. Is there dissatisfaction while asleep? When one sees through the deceit of self-consciousness, one returns to inherent peace and silence.

To sleep is to give up identification with name and form. Seeing everything as yourself is sleeping while awake. In other words, when everything that comes has gone, what remains is what I am.

Let this be your contemplation for today.

The Master said:

To what does "mine" refer? "Mine" is what belongs to me. But what belongs to me cannot be me. So what is required is to investigate what constitutes this "me" that is different from "mine".

We create the ideas of "inner" and "outer" by setting the body as the central point of reference. Yet, we fail to question the validity of this.

We know ourselves by the ideas we hold about ourselves. When we abandon all ideas about ourselves, we really get to know ourselves.

We overlook what is inherent in us and give our attention to what truly is not "ours".

We say that we see because we have eyes. This is, of itself, not true. A corpse has eyes, yet does not see.

Likewise, it can be said that we must have a brain in order to see, but here again the example of the corpse proves otherwise.

The sense organs know their respective sense objects and the brain knows the sense organs. But in the absence of the Being Knowing Energy, nothing is.

What I am is not at all affected by the actions, perceptions, thoughts and feelings that appear. As such, nothing need be done about them.

Let this be your contemplation for today.

The Master said:

What is real is real to everyone; what is false is always personal.

When "I" ceases to be, the notion of "mine" has no meaning. Embodiment is merely a temporary phenomenon that masks one's eternal nature.

When it becomes clear that one is not the body, there also ceases to be "others with bodies".

When subjectivity is unaffected by the coming and going of phenomena, what is left over is referred to as peace. Yet, one must make a sincere declaration: am I the subjectivity or am I an object?

Waking, dreaming, and sleeping pass before me. Something continuous exists throughout the three discontinuous phases. I am That.

What can wake up can fall asleep again. What never sleeps has no need for awakening.

Let us now return to the silence for a time.

Master Wu Hsin continued:

That which one is doesn't need enlightenment; it is only for that which one isn't.

Birth and death relate to the individual, and since the individual is a delusion, birth and death lose their meaning.

The I-idea is always seeking proofs of its validity. All "my's" are such attempts. The end of I is the end of ideas.

Investigation results in seeing that "you" cannot be located in either time or space, neither inside nor outside. This not-finding is the doorway to what one is.

The body is the clothing of Being Consciousness. Seen in this light, identification falls away.

Let us now return to the silence for a time.

Master Wu Hsin continued:

Most of those who come to Wu Hsin are desirous of improving their personal condition.

Had they realized that success here requires the giving up of all personal conditions, they would never have come.

This much cannot be overly stressed. The house becomes a prison when one can't leave it.

Wu Hsin advises to view the body as your house. You can come and go as you please.

It is only when you are identified with it that you are imprisoned.

Let this be your contemplation for today.

Today, the Master began:

Consciousness is the expression of the Absolute. The world is the expression of Consciousness.

Attending to the world is mind. Attending to attention itself is Being

The latter is the only so-called practice that is needed.

When the self directs its attention to the Self, the self dissolves into the Self, taking with it all its imaginations.

What remains is the Silence that cannot be disturbed by any amount of noise.

You can't walk towards It and you can't walk away from It. You are It.

Ponder this; more tomorrow.

Today, the Master began:

Regardless of the species, there is no "who" that is distinct from the organism. Naming every water buffalo on the rice farm doesn't make each an individual.

We create a world related to an erroneous subjective object, me.

All ideas of "who" are merely a product of human imagination, reinforced by memory of former imaginations.

Inquire: "What am I?"

Think on this deeply. Wu Hsin will speak again tomorrow.

The rains have been unrelenting and have created some hardships amongst us.

The Master entered the Great Hall and began:

What is realization? One regards as real that which is unreal. The cessation of this is realization. It need not be given; it is available to all in every moment.

One cannot clearly see the contents of a room filled with smoke. With the removal of the smoke, only then can one enjoy clarity.

Your view of the world is smoke-filled, so to speak. This smoke is comprised of "I" and other. Their removal is the requirement.

In life, we progress from the no-knowingness of an infant, to self consciousness, to the accumulation of concepts. This results in binge thinking and must be reversed.

It is impossible to fill a mind with Self that is already filled with myself. The emptying and subsequent refilling yields the Self without any sense of myself.

The idea of being an individual is the primary distortion of reality. From this, endless other distortions emerge. However, in the absence of imagination, it becomes clear that there is existence, but no individual existence.

Let this be your contemplation for today.

Today, the Master began:

The "I" is the conscious awareness of being in the present moment and having the authorship of actions.

Then there is the notion of "me", the personal identity, which is who you are based on all your past information and experiences. This is the story of who you are, the owner of all "my's". But both the "I", as actor, and the "me" are constructions.

Certainly we know that memories are always constructed, reinterpreted, reframed; so, information is reformatted to fit with a characterization. The sense of 'I,' and having free will is also constructed.

This "I" has meaning for us on three levels: the person thinks and feels "I", the touch of beingness is the experience of "I" without thinking, and the Ultimate is "I", without experiencing it.

This means that the Real which we are is always so already.

Let this be your contemplation for today.

The Master began:

Objective attention is the malady and subjective attention is the remedy.

When you are no longer someone, what remains?

So many ask Wu Hsin to prescribe a practice. What is there to be done?

It is like cooking a stew. Ingredients must be gathered, prepared and mixed together. Then the cooking process begins. It is only at a finger snap that the dish is deemed ready.

In the same way, all practices are mere preparation whereas the result of the preparation is sudden and spontaneous.

Using another image, the task is to fray the rope; the snapping happens in its own time.

Let us now return to the silence for a time.

Master Wu Hsin continued:

When we examine the notion "I am this", we observe that the "I am" is constant whereas the "this" is constantly changing. When the attention is moved from the latter to the former, one faces knowingness.

It is consciousness cognizing what appears in consciousness.

What you really are is that by which you know you are. You are the very consciousness through which the world is expressed.

Where would the picture be without the canvas on which it is painted? Consciousness is the wordless message "I am".

At its root, knowingness is the foundation of everything. In the absence of sugar, what can be made sweet?

Let this be your contemplation for today.

The Master began:

All questions belong to the mind and the mind belongs to the person. The end of the person is the end of questioning.

For as long as one is satisfied with the fruits of the world, this line of investigation will hold no appeal.

Although our image of ourselves changes over time, something subtle remains unchanged. Rabid pursuit of this yields a final understanding.

An individual dies only once. But if he chooses to die before he dies, then he will never die.

Yet, we continue to cling to our individuality, failing to realize that we are, in fact, the avatar of Conscious Being. When the shift occurs, it is from being the actor to being the witnessing of the action.

As water remains present between two successive waves, Conscious Being is present between any two successive appearances, be they mental or physical.

Let this be your contemplation for today.

The Master began:

Energy moving through water we call wave. Energy moving through air we call lightning. Energy moving through the body we call person.

Every "me" points to Me. Every "mine" points to Mine.

The arising of self consciousness produces a shadow-I seemingly apart from I Itself. This shadow-I is, in fact, the avatar of I Itself.

Gleaning the latter from the former is not difficult. Remove the mass of beliefs, interests, tastes, pretenses and reactions; what remains is I Itself.

Now, let us be silence.

Master Wu Hsin continued:

All experiences require the use of the senses except for the experience of being conscious.

As such, this Being Consciousness must be prior to the body and its sense organs.

All problems are personal, that is to say, they all arise from the concept of the person. Prior to "becoming a person", no problems existed.

Remembering and forgetting is always about some "other". One never remembers or forgets oneself.

Now, let us return to silence.

Master Wu Hsin continued:

I am is undeniable Truth. Anything that appends this "I am", such as I am this or I am that, is false.

I am not in a body; a body is in me.

If pressed to state a goal, I would say it is to be alive and conscious, but no longer self conscious.

If you seek for yourself outside of yourself, how can you ever find yourself?

Now, let us return to silence.

Master Wu Hsin continued:

Me can be deemed to be a physical object or a mental object. But it must never be taken to be the subject.

Most thought is merely the egoic micromanagement of "me". Recognition of this is a movement away from it.

Need anything be done in order to experience? Things need doing only when we desire to customize experience.

No investigation is required for objective knowledge. Investigation is only to bring the subjective to the fore.

Let this be your contemplation for today.

Master Wu Hsin entered the Great Hall, seated himself and began:

Personality gives us this sense of continuity. However, it inhibits any identification with the totality of life.

Presence is that which distinguishes between being engaged in thought and being aware of one's engagement in thought.

Body consciousness is Consciousness conscious of the body that hosts it. The loss of body consciousness is in no way the loss of Consciousness.

Then the Master rose and departed.

Master Wu Hsin started:

Having transformed the information gathered through the five senses into the world, one sees that world as objects which are not oneself, and one becomes distracted with likes and dislikes for those objects.

Such is the nature of confusion.

Life, as we describe it, is nothing more than an outgrowth of the self-consciousness.

In the final analysis, who is there to do anything?

All actions are initiated by the life force; its speech is mind. That which knows action, knows speech, is the consciousness. That which knows consciousness is that which is antecedent Oneness, the Absolute.

Insofar as this is so, what needs to be accomplished?

Apperceive what is the presiding principle by which you know you are and by which you perceive everything else.

That is all.

Now, spend the balance of the day in silence.

Master Wu Hsin started:

A cube of ice placed into water has temporary existence.

Before it acquired the form, it was water. It then took form for a while and ultimately merges back into its source.

Yet at no time was the ice cube separate from water, despite the fact that it may seem so.

In this regard, one must come to discern What-Is from what seems to be.

Be silent for a time.

Wu Hsin continued:

That one exists in the absence of thought is clear and obvious.

As such, You, the essential you, are not a thought but prior to any.

Individuality is the prism through which the world becomes distorted.

This is the case because the world is represented as how it relates to "me".

Literally and figuratively, when the prism is removed, all becomes clear.

Now sit in the quietude.

Master Wu Hsin continued:

The two great delusions are that life is controllable and that there is an entity, me, who can exercise said control.

But if we cannot even control the thoughts that appear to us, how can we possibly believe that we can control what occurs to us?

That is enough for today.

Wu Hsin started:

All there is, is the total functioning of consciousness within the manifestation.

There are no individuals, only billions of forms through which the functioning occurs. The totality is constant, while the functioning parts come and go.

Whatever one is must be present always. All else are add-ons, the "what I am" added to the "I am".

When you are sleeping deeply, without any dreams, you are not associated with your body or your mind. Who or what is this "you" that is not associated?

This investigation is about no longer fixating.

It is about removing one's acquisitions so that all one is left with is what one arrived with.

Ponder this; more tomorrow.

Wu Hsin started:

Relinquish all preoccupation with what was, or shall be. All one must know, is What-Is.

Because What-Is is ineffable, the mind cannot think about it. Its fallback position, is to therefore think about this world of temporal, transient, appearances.

The world is only the ocean of the mind, revealed in consciousness.

We create our world, populate it with friends and enemies, and then experience an ever-changing stream of psycho-physiological events.

As it is impossible for me to know what it is like to be another, it is equally impossible for me to comprehend another's world.

You have made your world; now, you can re-make it.

Go out and do so.

With that, he rose and walked out.

Master Wu Hsin started:

Imagine a place where you have never been. I can tell you about it, but that is only a description. I can present you with images of it but that only enhances the description.

This place is something that can only be known when it is experienced.

In a way, it is the same with Consciousness except that it can only be experienced by being consciousness; not consciousness of this or that. Being Consciousness.

When you are alive and conscious, but no longer self-conscious, you have returned to that place prior to the birth of personhood.

Investigate the reality of what you claim as "I".

The moment the "I" is proven to be a mere mental construction, then its polarity, the world that rises and sets alongside it, must also be unreal.

Now, who is it who knows that the "I" is unreal?

This knowledge within you that knows the "I" is unreal, that knowledge which knows change, must itself be changeless, unmoving and permanent.

Ponder this; more tomorrow.

The Master sat himself and said:

What is the world? The world is objective phenomena.

What knows the world? The world is known by the formless subjective.

As such, there are only the two: the formless subjective and the objective phenomena. Another name for the formless subjective is consciousness.

Where is the world located?

Consciousness turned toward the world is mind. The world appears in, and is therefore located in, the mind.

The entanglement between the formless subjective and objective phenomena is made via the conceptual individual entity, functioning as the go-between.

All thoughts and actions are to be understood as the effects of the life force received and transmitted through the inert body.

In this sense, the Self is what remains when you remove the self.

Unmanifest, I am the potentiality wherefrom manifestation is actualized.

Ponder this; more tomorrow.

The Master began:

Wakefulness ends, I am.

Dreaming ends, yet I am.

Dreamless sleep ends, yet I am.

Each repeats and, all the while, I am.

Everything is momentary; each experience serves as a subtle reminder that I am.

I-am without form is the Supreme; with form, it is Wu Hsin and the world.

Can you quiet yourself long enough to see yourself?

The Master clapped his hands and left the Hall.

The Master began:

Before any beginning, there was only Dynamic Potentiality. When actualized, this manifests into Dynamic Intelligent Energy expressing itself as the body and the world.

The body is an instrument necessary for consciousness to perceive its objective manifestation.

The sole problem is the identification resulting in the imagined concept of an independent, autonomous entity which creates the seeming actor, thus making the actions one's own.

Phenomena are integrally latent in noumenon. When there is manifestation of the Absolute as separate phenomenal objects, there arises a subject which perceives and cognizes and an object which is perceived and cognized.

The key is that both the cognizer-subject and the cognized-object are interdependent and can only exist in the consciousness in which the manifestation process occurs.

We can only exist as one another's objects to the seeming subject-cognizer. From here, the mind reifies the seeming subject-cognizer, creating the entity cognizer which is considered to be the subjective function.

Expanding yet further, this entity assumes itself to be independent and autonomous with volition and choice.

Yet, all the while this play is going on, what we are, the Absolute manifested as the totality of phenomena, continues unchanged.

Ponder this; more tomorrow.

The Master began:

During the course of your life, how many identities have you claimed as your own? Where are they now?

You are now confronted with a pivotal choice: living tossed about in various states or abiding in the Stateless. Living in humanity vis-a-vis living in divinity.

Because no one has ever told you that you had this choice, you've never looked at it before.

There is the I-am-this, or waking, state. Then here is the I-am-another-this, or dream state. Finally, there is the contentless state of deep sleep. This cycles repeatedly.

Just as an open space becomes three parts when two partition walls are erected in its midst, so when the two kinds of body-identification, namely the waking-body and the dream-body, are imagined, the unitary Self appears to become three states, that of waking, dream and sleep.

The self-attention, which goes on continuously, must switch over to Self-attention. The living in divinity is the result.

Ponder this; more tomorrow.

Master Wu Hsin began:

We miss the actual by lack of attention and create distortions by excessive imagination.

Understand that without Being there is nothing.

All knowledge is about Being.

Wrong ideas about Being lead to dissatisfaction and unhappiness, whereas right ones lead to freedom and happiness

Likewise, understand that Consciousness illuminates.

Everything perceived is first illuminated by Consciousness.

Even when there is nothing to be perceived, Consciousness is present.

Now, let there be silence.

Master Wu Hsin continued:

The habitual reference to a false center must end.

You have dedicated decades to building a prison for yourself. Can you not find a few moments to begin to tear it down?

The experiences you have in one state do not follow you into another state. Therefore, they cannot be part of your essential self.

You take yourself to be that which events happen to. Cease to be the object and become the subject of all that happens.

Merely see yourself as the illuminant of everything.

Now, let there be silence.

Master Wu Hsin continued:

Wholeness is not a state; states come and go.

Wholeness is holiness, absolute presence and relative absence.

"I will be" is prior to differentiation.

It is the Dynamic Potentiality, preceding all states, including the "I am" state.

Nothing more need be said today.

Ponder this; more tomorrow.

Master Wu Hsin began:

The body is an inert thing. It is like a kite that flies when the wind blows yet cannot function when the power is not available.

That which animates the body is really all that I speak about. What is that? It is life energy plus consciousness.

The brain and the body cannot be treated as separate. They are a singular, integrated whole.

The personality is how the brain "acts" via the body. Don't become distracted by the notion of "mind". Mind equals brain process; it's another object of perception.

We say that the moon shines in the same way as we say that there is a person that acts. Yet, it is not that the moon is shining. Rather, it is merely reflecting the light of the sun.

Persons, too, are only the reflected light of That which shines on them and provides their support.

Ponder these words; more tomorrow.

Master Wu Hsin began:

Fifty feet below the ocean's surface, no waves can be discerned.
Therefore, to transcend the waves of the world, diving deep is
necessary.

Any movement of consciousness toward the phenomenal is
equivalent to a movement away from what is real. The Real is
attained by a movement of consciousness in the direction opposite
from that by which the phenomenon is experienced.

Go behind all experience to that which is aware of the experience,
and that which ties the multiplicities of experience into the unity of
one whole. This center is that which I am.

Likewise, the strength of the sunlight has no relevance to those who
live in caves.

The invitation of Wu Hsin is to step outside.

Let all sit in silence.

Master Wu Hsin continued:

Awakening in the morning begins the narrative of a "you in the world". Dreaming begins another narrative of a "different you in a different world". Both seem completely real in their moment.

But what distinguishes the real from mere appearance is continuity.

What comes and goes is the very definition of appearance.

We say it is real while it is there; but can we say it is real when it is not there?

The finite is nothing other than the expression of the Infinite. Whatever is perceived is continuously created and destroyed. Consciousness is the medium in which this occurs.

Consciousness witnesses the world whereas the Absolute witnesses consciousness.

Ponder these words; more tomorrow.

Master Wu Hsin began:

The body is the instrument of consciousness and consciousness is the instrument of the Unmanifest made manifest.

Each species has a role in the functioning of consciousness.

Every living thing, every instrument, acts in accordance with the inherent nature of its species.

It is inherent in humans that self-consciousness arise.

Be total in oneself; discern that the individual and its world are a singular whole.

Let all sit in silence.

Master Wu Hsin continued:

As long as you consider yourself to be a body, then the world seems to be external to it.

What is the world other than a superimposition of a creation of the mind? The world is merely a spontaneous appearance. The one who perceives the appearance is included in it as a character, nothing more.

The mind cannot discern the unreality of its projection while it remains immersed in it. It does not understand its cravings for content and variety. If it did, it's pursuit of the transient would end.

Since the entirety of the world is contained in the mind, changing the mind changes the world.

Let all sit in silence.

Master Wu Hsin continued:

In one sense, intellect creates the ego as a secondary survival system. Thus the self-conscious life is born. It is entirely reflexive, nothing more than stimulus-response.

In a different sense, this ego or micro I-am functions as the bridge between the inert, insentient body and the macro I-am, consciousness, the manifestation of the Absolute.

Either way, the individual is a habitual point of view. It is memory, the past only.

What you know about yourself is what you remember about yourself. Take a minute a check; see if what you call the "person" is anything more than the set of images in memory.

The identification with the body is no different than the dog's identification with the body. If it is not transcended, one is no better than a dog. In fact, one is worse off since the dog is not plagued by worry, guilt, regret, etc.

Ponder these words; more tomorrow.

Master Wu Hsin began:

There is much talk about realization or self realization.

To realize is to make something real, is it not? How do you go about making what is already real real? We seek to make it real because we presuppose its absence.

This is the root error. If it is not here now, then it lacks permanence. Haven't you had enough of chasing after the impermanent?

Attention liberates. From moment to moment, you chose what you attend to. If you choose the outflow of the mind or the appearance of the world, you take them to be real.

But neither can take you to the Real.

Let all sit in silence.

Master Wu Hsin continued:

Imagine a world without humans. It has birds and cows, cats and dogs, and hundreds of thousands of other organisms. Each behaves according to its nature.

There is not a single person.

Now introduce humans into the mix. They too, behave according to their nature.

Seeing this mix still devoid of a single person is clarity of sight.

Let all sit in silence.

Master Wu Hsin continued:

The idea of a permanent self is a conceptual fiction.

Too, adopting such a view leads to accepting the validity of notions such as 'I,' 'me,' and 'mine' with deleterious effects for well being.

In that sense, attachment to such a fictional 'I' is the root cause of a range of negative emotions, including selfishness, craving, hatred, conceit, and ill-will.

What is the true condition is that there is no subject that sees the other as an object.

There is only seeing, which is functioning as an aspect of the Potentiality.

Ponder these words; more tomorrow.

Master Wu Hsin began:

There is only an appearance of there being many different objects.

This appearance is one that is generated by the subjective mind, which holds itself in isolation from everything that it perceives as being outside of itself.

The world one experiences is tailored by one's beliefs.

How can it possibly be claimed to be real?

Let all sit in silence.

Master Wu Hsin continued

"To know the world, you remove your attention from its support.

To know the support, you remove attention from the world.

The preoccupation with the world is merely one's love of narrative. Cease all worry regarding the world.

Until you can admit that the world is your own creation, you need not worry about the world.

Once you make the admission, the world takes care of itself.

Ponder this; more tomorrow.

Wu Hsin said:

"To continue, the process of phenomenal manifestation depends on the media of space and time.

In the absence of space, no object's volume could become apparent.

Likewise, in the absence of time, no thing could be perceived without the duration necessary to make the object perceivable.

The process of phenomenal manifestation, therefore, takes place in this unique media.
Objects become appearances in consciousness.

They are perceived and cognized by consciousness, through an instrument that serves as its host.

This host is the body.

Therefore, consciousness becomes embodied within duality in order to perceive its diverse expressions.

Ponder this; more tomorrow.

Master Wu Hsin began:

You are not your thoughts.

The thoughts come to you in the same way that rain falls on you.

Nor are you a thinker.

In the absence of thought, you remain.

You are not a doer, an actor.

In the absence of action, you remain.

Let all sit in silence.

Master Wu Hsin continued:

When you direct attention to how you, the organism, function and behave, it gradually becomes clear that most of the function and behavior is mechanical and automatic.

You begin to realize that the person you have taken yourself to be is a fiction.

This person is like the music produced by the instrument. Or it could be stated that like the tartness in a lime or the sweetness of honey, the person is merely the quality or expression of the organism.

The individual is really a series of interconnected processes working together that give the appearance of being a single, separated whole.

Let all sit in silence.

Master Wu Hsin continued:

Do we possess an individual self or soul that is separate from our physical biology or are we simply an enormously complex biological network that mechanically produces our hopes, aspirations, dreams, desires, humor, and passions?

A name and a form are merely an address.

It is there, like your shadow is there in daylight. Give it the same attention that you give to your shadow.

What occupies the address is what is important. When you are alive and conscious, but no longer self-conscious, your days of personhood will have ended.

Ponder this; more tomorrow.

Master Wu Hsin began:

Consciousness is immovable omnipresence.

It goes to nothing, everything comes to it.

When beckoned, time comes, space comes, here and now begin.

Consciousness is no thing.

This is difficult to grasp because your frame of reference is of things.

Presently, you are like the moon, believing your light is your own.

Identity is the "who I am" whereas personality is the "how I am".

Body, senses and mind are not always with you.

Therefore they are not integral to the essence.

It is only self consciousness that sleeps and awakens and it is not that which decides to sleep and awaken.

It arises and sets outside of its own control.

Body identification is a habit; as it had a beginning, it can have an end.

Ponder this; more tomorrow.

Master Wu Hsin began:

Root mind is comprised of I-am and There-is.

Essential Nature, Conscious Being, is prior to these.

Conceptual mind is I-am-this and There-is-that.

The flaw is that we allowed conceptual mind to define what is real.

Yet, what is real is prior to concepts of any kind.

There is no me and you.

There is only Me as you.

There is only Me as this, as that.

There is only Me.

Ponder this; more tomorrow.

Master Wu Hsin began:

The entire manifestation exists only in consciousness.

The process would be that consciousness arises out of Awareness.

The Actuality appears from the Great Potential, as would be its nature.

In consciousness the world appears and disappears.

Consciousness is the witnessing of whatever happens.

Let us be clear.

Wu Hsin is not saying that the world does not exist.

It exists, but solely as an appearance in consciousness.

In that regard, its so called existence is temporal.

The world can be said to appear, but not be.

Ponder this; more tomorrow.

Master Wu Hsin began:

Wu Hsin declares "I am' alone is; and not "I am so and so", or "I am such and such".

Particularized existence is a gross reduction of What-Is.

When we give up all thoughts except for "I am", are we not peaceful?

Now give up even the "I am" thought and see what remains.

Ponder this; more tomorrow.

The Master entered and sat himself when disciple Qin Qing approached, made his salutation and then began:

"Master, I have some questions"..............

Wu Hsin interrupted him.

All questions are premature at his time.

It is indicative that your consideration of my words has not been sufficient in either depth or duration.

When the contemplation has been full and complete, there will be no questions.

Entrust these matters to silence.

Silence is the great solvent that dissolves all questions

He then rose, clapped his hands together and said:

Ponder this; more tomorrow.

Master Wu Hsin began:

Let us continue this inquiry into the world.

The world is nothing but perceptions, thoughts, intuitions and feelings.

Where do they appear?

Where does experience happen?

When you perceive an elephant, the perception is held in your mind.

The weight of the elephant does not place any strain on the mind, because it is only an image.

In this regard, all perceptions are mere images.

An evidence based inquiry reveals the insubstantiality of it all.

It then becomes clear and obvious.

First listen to me.

Think over it deeply and imbibe it. Constantly think about it.

This brings you closer to ending your climbing up the stairs of endless doubt.

Ponder this; more tomorrow.

The Master began:

The first card in the house built of cards is self consciousness, the thought "I am this body". What most take for this "I" is solely identity plus personality.

The body and world rises only when the mind rises, exists only so long as the mind exists, and vanishes when the mind sets.

Therefore, is there a world apart from the mind?

Without the body, the world does not exist.

You have confused yourself with your uniform.

That which knows itself is embodied in the organism.

The body is the instrument through which Consciousness experiences its manifestation.

It is the window of Consciousness, so to speak.

This manifestation requires the media of time and space. Consciousness resides outside of both and is therefore not knowable as some thing to be known.

Ponder this; more tomorrow.

The Master began:

The true state of Being remains empty, fixed and silent.

All movement occurs in it.

But we ignore the former and focus solely on the latter.

However, we forget that the latter is impossible without the former.

When every "this" and "that" has been absorbed into "I", we see things as they really are.

Ponder this; more tomorrow.

The Master began:

The person is the Primary Distortion.

Therefore, anything experienced through the person must be distorted.

This person is a shadow of the Self.

We refer to it as my self.

When we ask "How do I take care of this body?", we infer a relationship between the "I" and the body.

Therefore, they are not the same.

It is clear that the body is an object.

The issue for investigation is "What is this 'I'?"

Ponder these words; more tomorrow.

Master Wu Hsin began:

Wherever one goes, "I" is always present.

What is this "I"?

This is the basis for the investigation.

However, the investigation must not start out looking for what we expect to find or for what we're told we'll find or for what we hope to find.

In that regard, we cannot define the target to be that which we have successfully hit.

Now stay silent.

Wu Hsin broke the silence.

The core confusion is the entanglement of Knowing with known actions of personality.

For true awakening, witness and witnessed must resolve into Witnessing.

Until then, duality continues.

Understand that personality is objectively observable; it can be discerned via the observation of behavior.

That which observes it is not it.

In that regard, the attention must move from the objective to the subjective for all to be made clear.

By way of further clarification, witnessing is not an experience.

Witnessing is the registration of the presence or the absence of experience.

In it, everything that happens is registered, including the happening referred to as "me".

Ponder these words; more tomorrow.

Master Wu Hsin began:

Conscious Existence is one's natural condition.

So-called states are add-ons to it.

Conscious Existence plus waking, we call waking.

Conscious Existence plus sleep, we call sleep and Conscious Existence plus dream, we call dream.

Conscious Existence emerges from the Primordial and returns to It.

It arises and sets with time and space.

It is therefore important not to lose sight of the fact that even Conscious Existence is not the final destination.

In that regard, any notion of attainment contains an inherent flaw: there is nothing to attain.

You can't attain what you already have.

Ponder these words; more tomorrow.

Master Wu Hsin began:

As long as one believes that they are finite and temporary, then death is their logical outcome. But what is death to the Infinite Timeless?

Therefore, there should be no preoccupation with the notion of an afterlife.

Death is the content of the afterlife. Our interests must focus on the after-death.

We want to transition from believing in our frail mortality to being immortal.

Seeing one's blindness is the first step in restoring this clarity of vision.

Now, be silent.

After a time, the Master continued:

Every thing is attached to "I".

Detaching every thing from "I" allows what remains to fully reside in that one true, anterior nature which is the source of all worlds and the seeming selves contained therein.

When there is a commitment to the investigation, one's personal chaos becomes one's question insofar as one must ask "Whose chaos is this?"

It should not be misunderstood to be an exchange of bad for good or sadness for happiness. These are two sides of the same coin.

The intended outcome of the investigation is to throw away the coin.

Ponder these words; more tomorrow.

Master Wu Hsin began:

The true state of Being remains empty, fixed and silent; all movement occurs in it.

But we ignore the former and focus solely on the latter, forgetting that the latter is impossible without the former.

What-Is is This-Here-Now, Conscious Being.

Any This-Here-Now that refers to appearances soon becomes That-There-Then and is revealed to be false.

Likewise, the time bound false self points back to the Eternal Self.

When every "this" and "that" has been absorbed into "That", we see things as they really are.

Ponder these words; more tomorrow.

The Master said:

Only I am.

The dualities of seer and seen resolve into Seeing; hearer and heard into Hearing, etc.

All perceivers and perceptions, all conceivers and conceptions, are objects only.

That which cognizes the object assumes that it is the subject of the cognition for other objects, in a world external to itself, and this cognizing subject regards its pseudo-subjectivity as constituting an independent, autonomous entity.

This is the core delusion from which the deluded world view arises.

The most treacherous aspect of the I/not-I duality is that it is mistaken for actuality.

To frame questions within this context frames questions that are inherently flawed. Answers to such questions must therefore also be flawed.

Ponder these words; more tomorrow.

The Master said:

We consider as real anything that is perceptible to the senses, and yet every imaginable thing that is sensorially perceptible must pass through an interpretation by the mind before it is cognized.

Anything that is cognized in this fashion is obviously only an appearance in the consciousness of the cognizer.

As such, all phenomena are mere appearances in space-time, perceived in consciousness.

Consciousness experiences its expressions thru the body which is one of its expressions.

In the absence of a body, can we speak of conscious experience?

Ponder these words; more tomorrow.

The Master said:

I am the origin and terminus of every thought, of every movement, as waves arise and end in water.

As every wave occurs in the ocean, all phenomena occur in me.

Just as perception illuminates objects, I am that which illuminates perception.

Whatever appears can only appear because I am. Every appearance points back to this.

Every sound occurs against the background of silence.

When the sound is finished, the silence remains. Look for it.

Every object occurs against the background of empty space.

When the object is finished, the space remains. Look for it.

Ponder these words; more tomorrow.

The Master said:

The world is nothing other than a representation of sensation. Repeating sensations create the artifact referred to as "the known". These are the sensations that you re-call.

In no small way, what you see, hear, feel, and think is based on what you expect to see, hear, feel, and think. In turn, your expectations are based on all your re-calls.

Things are objects in time and space and thoughts are objects in time. Constrained by these, how do you propose to see That which is unconstrained?

Begin by seeing your unawareness of your unawareness. Then, establish an outpost of observation outside of your personality and identity.

What you are now is what you've always been. You are that beingness.................you are.

Yet, even this Beingness, the actualization of the Potentiality, is time-bound too. All the forms, all the names, only exist in this beingness, when you are.

Lacking the moment-to-moment awareness that "you are" doesn't mean that you are not. It only means that your attention is elsewhere. So, bring it back:

What is the difference between the eyes of a statue and your own?

Both are eyes, yet some power facilitates sight in you but not in the statue. Turn your attention toward that Power, toward That.

Ponder these words; more tomorrow.

The Master said:

Enlightenment or self-realization is the apperception of an existence transcending the body.

The person does not exist apart from the world. The world does not exist apart from the body.

The body does not exist apart from the mind. The mind does not exist apart from Consciousness; and Consciousness does not exist apart from Existence.

Seeing this clearly is enlightenment.

All states seem real from a vantage point within the state.

It is only when one is outside the state, that one can evaluate the state's reality. For example, the dream is real within the dream. It is only outside dreaming that the dream can be said to be false.

In a similar sense, whatever can be known with the mind is a product of said mind. The mind does not reflect; it distorts.

One who knows that the world is not as it appears yet refuses to investigate further is guilty of willful blindness.

Ponder these words; more tomorrow.

The Master said:

In dim light, many things are seen incorrectly.

When the pure light of consciousness is dimmed by mentation, we cannot experience reality. When we change the way we look at things, things change.

If we relinquish the notion of three states, that is waking, dreaming and dreamless sleep, and replace it with the notion of One State on which these three appear and disappear, everything takes on new meaning.

Just as friction is required to begin a fire, likewise friction is required for the attainment of clarity.

This friction is brought about by investigation of the validity of one's beliefs. It is not so much that the truth is gained as it is that the false is lost.

Ponder these words; more tomorrow.

The Master said:

If one is sincere in seeking to be free, one must free oneself from these beliefs and from all hearsay that has been acquired and taken to be fact. Otherwise, that which we are attached to binds us.

The foundational or root attachment is to the idea that I am an object.

Do we possess an individual self or soul that is separate from our physical biology or are we simply an enormously complex biological network that mechanically produces our hopes, aspirations, dreams, desires, humor, and passions?

A name is merely an address. What occupies the address is what is important. When you are alive and conscious, but no longer self-conscious, your days of personhood will have ended.

The person may continue to be there, like your shadow is there. But it is seen for what it really is.

Ponder, then ponder more.

The Master said:

Egos are different but I-am is Oneness Itself.

Rest in I-am and ego loses its hold.

Ego means "I am this".

Understanding means "I am That".

Ego will never leave you.

Therefore, you must leave it.

You do so by ceasing to make it the focus of your attention.

A fish has no idea what water is like because it has nothing to compare it to.

It is only when we move away from personality that we can see it for what it is and what it isn't.

Ponder these words; more tomorrow.

Master Wu Hsin said:

How can an illusory "self" do anything to find reality when it is itself the obstacle to its realization and any effort to end itself only strengthens its seeming selfhood?

No amount of cleaning can make a wall white, as long as one looks at it through tinted glasses.

The individual mind is akin to the tinted glasses.

Self consciousness is the source of all dissatisfaction.

When consciousness is redirected away from the personal, dissatisfaction ceases.

Now, be quiet.

Master Wu Hsin said:

Words can only take you to the limits of words. Words are not facts, they only serve to point to them.

Where words end, is the borderline to reality. You cross it at your own risk, because once crossed, the seeming you is no longer.

It's all conceptual. You look at a log cabin and say "house" and I say "wood". Is one more right than the other?

If Wu Hsin goes to Fujian, digs up some soil, puts it in a jar, and brings it home, can he show the jar when friends ask what Fujian is like?

Ponder this, more tomorrow.

Master Wu Hsin continued his discoursing:

All ideas of responsibility require someone to be responsible.

To say it another way, an individual's purpose in life is to transcend individuality.

You can only experience ideas about yourself.

You cannot experience yourself because what you are is so subtle that it cannot be experienced.

Now, more quiet.

Master Wu Hsin said:

The traits you acquire over a lifetime, the good and the bad, are not you. They are yours.

Similarly, the mind, that lifetime's worth of impressions one has collected, is also yours.

To discern the "you" in every "yours" is clarity.

The truth is that the anterior-most I is lighter than air.

The only reason we feel earthbound is because we are holding on to something.

That thing is "me".

Stay quiet and ponder this.

Master Wu Hsin continued:

We can study the function and behavior of any organism. Why is it that only in humans do we create the concept of a person?

The person is like the music produced by the instrument.

The situation as it presents itself is that there is an organism and an entity in the organism whose thoughts, feelings, and actions are referenced as "the person".

What we are therefore suggesting is that we are possessed by the entity.

Even if this notion was left unchallenged, it begs the questions: "Where does the entity come from?"

Stay quiet and ponder this.

Master Wu Hsin continued:

How many are there who are interested in a life that is beyond the identification with the brain in the body?

When you are asleep and dreaming, your eyes are closed, but you're having full, rich visual experience —because it's the same process of running inside, and then you believe that you are seeing.

One of the seductive aspects of a dream is that it does not allow one to doubt its reality.

Don't be deceived.

There is Functioning and the Perceiving of the Functioning. The seen is discontinuous while that which sees stands outside of time.

Tomorrow Wu Hsin will rest.

Master Wu Hsin said:

Consciousness arises spontaneously out of Pure Potentiality, noumenon.

This spontaneous arising brings about the sense of presence, of existence.

It results in the arising of the phenomenal manifestation in consciousness, appearing as subject and object.

Unity has been split into duality.

The manifestation requires the creation of "space" and "time": "space" in which the objects could be extended, and "time" in which the phenomenal images could be perceived, cognized and measured in terms of the duration of existence.

This is the way of things; ponder this.

The Master began to speak:

Illusion can be accepted to be part of the totality of reality only when it is recognized as illusion.

Everything happens spontaneously without some grand plan.

The flight of swans is reflected in the lake's water, but the birds do not intend to make a reflection, nor does the water intend to reflect the flight of the birds.

Our senses readily perceive diversity but fail to discern the unity in diversity.

In much the same way, it is only our minds that stand between us and our god.

When imagination ceases, unity is self evident.

Anything you try to become is a movement away from what you already are.

All attempts at attainment are egoic, an attempt to reinforce what is in fact a fragmentation.

As water need not seek to attain wetness, one need not seek to attain what one already is.

Why not take "you are not what you appear to be" as a working theory, play with it continuously and then evaluate the result?

He then rose and left the Hall.

Master Wu Hsin said:

Today, Wu Hsin will be brief.

He tells everyone the same thing: "Your fundamental premises are flawed. Until you correct them, Wu Hsin cannot help you.

Once you correct them, you are already beyond the need for my or anyone else's help".

He then rose and left the Hall.

Master Wu Hsin said:

Presence is not a decision.

Presence is Being, not being here now. No effort is required to be.

Don't pollute this beingness, your knowledge that you are, I-am.

The pollution is adding to it; I am this, I am that. This is the source of the dissatisfactions and troubles.

Bar the imaginary.

The mind can destroy its inventions, given the proper circumstances. Whatever is temporary is fathered by the imagination.

See that only what is false strives for continuity. What is true has no concern for continuity because what is true is forever.

The outcome is pure mind. Not being constrained by any taint of self-consciousness, it has nothing separate from itself and is therefore only consciousness.

Ponder this, more tomorrow.

Master Wu Hsin said:

The Being Knowing Energy manifests.

Afterward, conceptions and perceptions appear. We take them to be "outside" and this is a fundamental error. All appears inside the Being Knowing Energy.

The waking state represents diversity in manifestation.

The dream state reveals that diversity is derived from a single source. The deep sleep state reveals said source and is not different from object-free consciousness.

The three states come and go; That which knows them does not.

That eternal principle which witnesses everything and the absence of everything is shaped like the wind, colored like the sky; how can it be described?

Ponder this, more tomorrow.

Master Wu Hsin said:

When Wu Hsin declares that we are immaterial, he is not being disrespectful.

Wu Hsin is saying that we are not matter and, as such, do not go through what matter goes through: origination, growth, decay and dissolution.

We are so preoccupied with what the body and the mind are doing. Yet, neither is the true self.

The ego chases after continuity, after perpetuity. In fact, it is seeking to return to the perpetuity from which it emerged.

We fear being alone as it is experienced as one step before not-being. Yet, for those who see the unity of all things, aloneness has no meaning.

Ponder this, more tomorrow.

Master Wu Hsin said:

Something is lost when you stop thinking, and that something is "you."

The person was not there before you were born, nor will it be there after you die.

Instead of struggling with the person, why not leave the personal altogether?

It does not mean the extinction of the person; it means only seeing it in right perspective.

Even if it is only for a single second, the experience of "no you" has the power to be life altering.

It is the very transcendence of the twin prisons of past and future.

Ponder this, more tomorrow.

Master Wu Hsin said:

Wu Hsin cannot help anyone become realized because he can't help anyone become what they already are.

Thought obscures the essential nature. Absent thought, Conscious Being shines.

There are some who fear having no thoughts, They fear they will fall apart or dissolve. But the absence of thought need not be feared.

If you know you are a man, you don't cease to be a man in the absence of thought.

Be silent and ponder this until Wu Hsin returns.

Master Wu Hsin continued:

Stillness and sensitivity facilitate the sensation of Conscious Presence in the body.

One perceives objects through the senses.

One perceives the senses through the mind.

What is it that perceives the mind?

The mind is not anything in itself. It is a function, a process. When thought and feeling are absent, the mind cannot be said to exist.

Therefore, what perceives the mind is only Consciousness.

This is the truth of Wu Hsin.

Consider this; more tomorrow.

The Master walked into the Hall, turned toward the group and said:

Consciousness turned outward is mind; mind turned inward is consciousness.

The preoccupation with the objective must be replaced with a preoccupation with the Subject. Instantly, everything clarifies.

Nothing more need be said today.

With that, the Master departed from the Hall.

More Questions Answered

Q: How can I maintain presence?
A: Presence is the absence of yourself. That which is, is as it is. It transcends the spoken word and is beyond all attempts at description.

Q: I have never experienced bliss. What is it, Master?
A: Bliss is the pure joy and contentment of Being Conscious.

Q: What remains when I have transcended my individuality?
A: What cannot come and cannot go remains.

Q: Master Wu Hsin, how can this one become enlightened?
A: All becoming is personal. From the impersonal, there is nothing to become. As such, there is no such thing as enlightenment except for the one who creates the need for it.

Q: Master, my problems overwhelm me. I cannot make myself quiet. There is no progress. What do you advise?
A: All problems are resolved when you resolve yourself. What am I really? Draw the distinction between having a body and being a body. See that whatever you perceive, whatever you think about, comes to you.
It is not you.
See that there is nothing to get. It is already present. All ideas about progress serve the mind only.
What progress is required to go from here to here?

Q: How may I get the experience of the Unchanging that you speak about?
A: Experience requires change. As such, the Unchanging cannot be experienced.
Experiencing, an experiencer, and that which is experienced all emerge from the same source and are essentially One.
In that sense, you are the "I," you are the "I am," and you are the world.

Q: Master, my understanding remains incomplete. What must I see that I am not seeing?
A: Whereas seeking understanding is a noble enterprise, the higher is seeking the cessation of misunderstanding.

Consider a hole. Dirt was removed to make it. Yet the space was there before and after the removal of the dirt. So, what is to be realized?

Only what is imaginary requires realization. The removal of the imaginary is sufficient. When that is accomplished, where is the need for further realizations?

Q: Master Wu Hsin, I cannot be with you every day. Am I doomed to failure?

A: Having the complete support of the Inner Teacher in every moment, there is no absolute mandate for an Outer Teacher.

My words can only take you to the limitations of my words. Beyond this, you must go alone.

Q: If I fail to attain enlightenment in this life, how will I be re-born?

A: There should be no preoccupation with re-birth. What is key is the continuation of the investigation into the mythology of this birth. If you are not identified with the body, how can you die? If you cannot die, nothing is re-born.

Q: There is complete disharmony between my inner and outer worlds. How can I reconcile the two?

A: Why do you continue to take everything personally?

Understand that there is no entity or person as such. This also means there is no personal consciousness and no personal inner world nor outer world. All there is, is universal consciousness and its phenomena.

In this regard, true discrimination is between the seeming personal and What-Is.

Q: Master, how would you describe yourself?

A: I am, as always, nothing perceivable or definable. Because you believe that you have a body, you expect other bodies and they appear. You cannot locate me, I am the wind.

I am unchanging and continuous, remaining as such in all the states which are constantly changing. You are now thinking that you are the mind or the body which are both changing and transient. But you are unchanging and eternal. I discern this; you, as yet, do not.

Q: Master Wu Hsin, Mengshi teaches us to be indifferent, to not want anything. Is this too a valid path?

A: Not wanting is not indifference. Not wanting is having no preferences. It is welcoming whatever arrives.
Wu Hsin does not offer paths. What path will deliver you to where you already are?

Q: Master, how can I be what I perceive?
A: The naming of the perception always comes after the perceiving. In this way, it can be seen that consciousness precedes mind.
This "me" is the mind's representation of the sensations, thoughts, feelings, actions and reactions that appear to it. All else is another representation, the world. In that sense, the world is there only because this "you" is there.

Q: How can I develop a relationship with my inner being?
A: There are no opposites, only complements. Relationship exists in duality. In the non-dual what is to have relationship with what? There is no outer being to relate to any inner being. There is only Being.

Q: Master, please reveal to me that state which is before my consciousness.
A; Any knowledge that Wu Hsin conveys can only be in the consciousness. How can the consciousness hold any knowledge about that state which exists prior to its arrival? Take your pose in consciousness, as consciousness, and see the result.

Q: Master, I come to you in distress. I have no time for lengthy practices. Is there an alternative?
A: Yes there is. Everyone lives out of memory. Replace the old memories with the memory of the words of Wu Hsin and live in accordance with that.
Then, you cannot fail.

Q: Master Wu Hsin, what are the criteria for evaluating a teacher?
A: You see yourself as a body that can evaluate another body. Both sides of the argument are erroneous. To see clearly, your mind must be pure and unattached. Then you will answer your own question.

Q: I am most dissatisfied with my life. What can I do to bring about a change in it?

A: A whole new way of living is required. Living from memory and acting habitually, what can one expect to accomplish?

Q: Master, it is most obvious to me that the world is real. How can you argue that it is not real?
A: Who trained you in discerning the real? How were you trained? You simply accept what appears to be real. Wu Hsin challenges your acceptance.

Q: Master, can you instruct me how to find my god?
A: Yes, my son, it is quite easy. Look where you are not.

Q: Master, I listen to your every word and try to imbibe them. Yet, I remain unaware. What do you advise?
A: See that your sense of unawareness appears in Awareness Itself. How can you say that you are unaware of being aware?

Q: Master, how can I acquire the same clarity as Wu Hsin?
A: You seek to amuse us, do you not? How can you acquire what you already are?

Q: Master Wu Hsin, which path is best?
A: Regardless of the path one chooses, ultimately one must lose oneself in it. Those unwilling to be lost need not initiate the first step on any path.

Q: Master, is the world real or unreal?
A: Whether the world is real or not real is not the key issue. Rather, the focus must be on whether the person in the world is real or unreal.
Whatever the finding, it will apply to both the person and the world.
Q: What is self realization?
A: Self realization is identification with nothing. It can also be said that it is also identification with everything.
What it is not is identification with the particular.

Q: What is wrong with viewing the world from a personal point of view?
A: The person is momentary; in different moments, one manifests different persons.

The person has intermittent existence; it comes and it goes. When there is deep involvement in anything, the person is not there. Nor is it present in sleep.

The inquiry must be directed toward what is not intermittent, to what underlies and supports the intermittent. This is one's natural state, Conscious Being Energy.

Q: I desire to develop a posture of no-mind. How may I do this?
A: Until one reaches "no-person", no-mind cannot be claimed. The best way to annihilate the person is not to provide it with the energy of attention. In the absence of attention, it withers and dies.

Q: Master, my unhappiness continues. Where is the happiness that you promised?
A: All those things that man yearns for: God, happiness, peace................. can only be found where "you" is not.

Q: Master Wu Hsin, which holy books would you advise this one to read?
A: The teaching of the Master is the very essence of all the holy books. A Master's words and ten thousand books are the same.

Q: Master, yours is one of many different perspectives. How can I discern which is the correct one for me?
A: Do not lose yourself in the labyrinths of philosophy; instead, go straight to the Source from which they all rise.
Abide there; it is there that the philosophies lose their relevance.

Q: Will my questionable actions in my younger years adversely affect me now?
A: There isn't anything such as "someone's actions"; there are only occurrences, events. Events happen. Happenings don't require someone.
The thought to act and the act itself are an integral whole. The mind devises and the body executes.
Neither are yours.

Q: My efforts have not produced my desired results. Is my practice flawed?

A: Whatever it is you seemingly do, are, or experience, you are aware space, that onto which everything appears. Without the need to define, divide, categorize, describe, understand, explain or seek anything, simply be that relaxed openness that you are.
This is all the practice that is required.

Q: Master, my mind dominates my every moment. Is there any method for making it quiet?
A: When it is clear that you are not the mind, you will no longer be concerned with the mind's contents.
Until that time, refuse to provide this mind with the energy of attention.

Q: Master, how am I to be liberated?
A: Attention liberates. From moment to moment, you chose what you attend to.
If you choose the outflow of the mind or the appearance of the world, you take them to be real. But neither can take you to the Real. When you direct attention to how you, the organism, function and behave, it gradually becomes clear that most of the function and behavior is mechanical and automatic. You begin to realize that the person you have taken yourself to be is a fiction.

Q: My Master Wu Hsin, all this talk of the reality or unreality of the individual has me most confused. Can you provide me with guidance?
A: The question of the reality of the individual entity is rendered moot when we deny importance to the entity. Then, whether it is real or not no longer matters.
The understanding finally comes that "I" am never going to find the solution to the problem because "I" is the problem!
At that point, no doing is possible and all effort is to be surrendered.

Q: How can I rid myself of my fears?
A: All fear is, at its root, the fear of self-extinction. It is biological in nature and is only transcended when identification with the organism is transcended.

Q: Master, my progress is very slow. Can you help?

A: All notions of progress are for the individual only. No individual, no need for progress.

Q: Master Wu Hsin, my life is without meaning. Every day is only drudgery. How do I get beyond this?
A: All quests for meaning are egoic demands for relevance. Knowing itself to be insubstantial, it strives to attach substance to itself.
See this and be done with it.

Q: I feel separate from everything else. You say this is an illusion, yet the feeling remains.
A: Having a body is the source of all feelings of separation. Is it not our very skin that separates inside from outside?
One false idea fathers other false ideas.
Clarify the distinction between "I have a body" and "I am in the body". That which operates from and thru the body is what has a body.

Q: Why is it so difficult to discern all that is false?
A: It is the nature of the false that it appears real for a moment. It is the insistence on clinging to the false that makes the true so difficult to see.

Q: Master, is there an end to all this?
A: Yes; it ends when you are no longer interested in getting anything.

Q: Master, you teach that all this is mere illusion. How can I break free of it?
A: All conscious efforts to get rid of the illusion is part of the illusion. For as long as one is imprisoned by inattention and imagination, the illusion continues.
Trust in That which gave you the illusion to take it away.

Q: Master Wu Hsin, I have tried to see the flaw in believing myself to be only an actor in this play. Yet, nothing changes. What would you advise?
A: Whether or not you see yourself as the doer of anything does not affect what happens.

Just as you have done nothing to grow up from childhood, there is nothing that needs to be done to grow out of identification with the body/mind composite.

Q: Master, what is freedom?
A: Freedom is the absence of beliefs, opinions, and preferences. Illusion, like a cloud, cannot be discerned from the inside. Only when one steps out of it does it become clear. This is freedom.

Q: Master, why can I not see things as others see them?
A: It relates to the individual point of view.
According to the view of different onlookers, the same woman is considered to be wife, husband's sister, daughter-in-law, mother, and more. Yet, she does not at all undergo any change in her form.
When the view changes from the relative to the absolute, there is no further disagreement.

Q: Master Wu Hsin, why do you say that the body and the mind are not important?
A: Wu Hsin does not say so. The body and the mind are important to the total functioning.
However, what is more important than the body and the mind is that which knows the body and the mind, that which observes the total functioning.
It is on this that Wu Hsin asks that you place your attention.

Q: Master, when we speak of the seer, the seeing, and the seen, it is the seer that is the subject; is this not so?
A: No it is not. The seer is itself an object, the instrument of the Seeing which is the true subject.
Stated differently, there is the world, the individual and that which transcends both.

Q: Master, how do I rise above my body sense?
A: There is no further rising to be sought. The sense of being a body or being in a body has arisen.
Therefore, to rid oneself of it requires subsidence, sinking back into that which prevailed prior to the arising.

Q: Dearest Master, I have been unable to find what you sent me to look for. What should I do?
A: Wu Hsin never sent you looking. How can you find what is not perceivable nor conceivable?
You are already looking from that which we are looking for.
You are; this is undeniable. Don't hold to "I am this".
Abide as being without being anything in particular. This is Wu Hsin's instruction.

Q: My intellect fails me. I do not see what you see. Can you help me?
A: All the intellectuals task the mind to confirm what is beyond the mind.
How can failure not be the outcome of this?
You are just like space, insofar as space is the beginning and the end of everything. See this and you'll have seen all that needs seeing.

Q: Master Wu Hsin, can you teach me to transcend this world?
A: The world is no more real than the individual who sees it. Our experience of the whole world is nothing but our thoughts of it. These thoughts have no continuous existence. They vanish in an instant, replaced by others. The succession creates the illusion of continuity.
What is the world other than the sum of one's concepts?
When you know the truth about yourself, the world is transcended.

Q: Master Wu Hsin, your teaching is too complex for my simple mind. Must I resign myself to never gaining clear sight?
A: You are neither the body nor the mind, yet aware of both.
Remembering only this in every moment will propel you onward.

Q: Master, am I not the thinker of my thoughts?
A: One is the total space to which everything appears, in which everything appears, on which everything appears. There is no need for narratives.
There is no thinker of thoughts.
Thoughts appear and they are witnessed by That which witnesses the arising and setting of all phenomena, all these transient displays.

Q: Master, what is your instruction for destroying the mind?

A: No one has ever destroyed the mind by confronting it. When it no longer receives the energy of attention, it withers and dies.

Q: Master Wu Hsin, my problems go on. No sooner than I solve one, another appears. How can I break this cycle?
A: First realize that your problems exist in your waking state only. Explore that fully and all your answers will be rendered.

Q: Master, you have students who have been with you for a decade or more and yet they still have not attained? Is it because they have not fully surrendered to you?
A: Regardless of the form of one's efforts, sooner or later one's physical and mental resources will come to an end. What is to be done then?
Wu Hsin does not ask for any surrender to him.
The suggestion is that there be surrender to the words and allow them to go deeply and establish roots inside. What ensues is a natural process, not done by anyone.

Q: When will the world change for its betterment?
A: Whatever can be changed, can be changed again.
When the attention shifts to the Unchangeable, then what needs changing no longer has any importance.
Q: Master Wu Hsin: what is enlightenment? I have heard it is like this or like that. But I want to hear from you.
A: A baby chick's speculating about its shell never breaks the shell. Only pecking will do that.
Speculating about what enlightenment is like is the same. Suffice it to say that the You without the you is true; it is enlightenment.
The rest is fantasy.

Q: How can I rid myself of this identification with the body?
A: In essence, the question is "how to rid myself of myself"?
When you borrow a pot from your neighbor, you never refer to it as "mine". When you apperceive this body to be borrowed, you will never again call it "mine".

Q: What keeps me apart from God-consciousness?
A: The only thing standing between you and God-consciousness is your infatuation with the world.

A mere shift in attention is the only medicine needed.

Q: Master, how can I escape from this always present feeling of being a separate being in the world?
A: See that there is no separation without the individuality that creates it. In the absence of "me", how can there be "other than me"?

Q: How is it that you see matters differently than I do?
A: It is so obvious that you are not what you believe yourself to be. I will concede, however, that these beliefs provide you with the sense of continuity that is required to support the ideas of identity and personality.
The way I am, this identity and personality, is as it is only because the "I am" arises first.
The only thing that places limits on Being are these beliefs of your individuality. Assume the stance whereby you stabilize as the observing of the body-mind.
Then you will know there is no individual.
Rest in "I am and I know that I am"; this is common to all. Don't venture into "what I am" as this is the trap.

Q: My consciousness continues its restlessness. How may I make it quiet?
A: Consciousness is impersonal; there is no "my consciousness".
The form with a name is the window of Consciousness which It uses to look out onto its expressions.
Do not concern yourself with its activity; merely observe it.

Q: Master, my life is in turmoil. When will it end?
A: You are joking, are you not?
All that is lacking is acceptance. What is this acceptance?
The reconciliation of the conflict between the demands of Life and those of "my life" is acceptance.

Q: What must I do to see things clearly?
A: It is more than a mere exchange of concepts. Any exchange of concepts will not move you any closer to that space that is prior to all concepts.

What the sages for hundreds of years have understood has been developed in two ways: One way is they assimilated what they have been taught; they received it externally. The other way is it grew from inside, intuitively. This is apperception.

The two, when combined, cannot fail.

As you begin to go within, you will realize that you've always been within, projecting a seeming outside. But, truly, there's nowhere to go. Then, within and without lose all meaning............... and this is the end of mind; it is the end of questions.

Only the mind questions. That which one really is has no questions.

Q: Master, any peace of mind continues to elude me. What do you prescribe?

A: Peace of mind, no peace of mind............you are, regardless of either.

Q: Master Wu Hsin, please give me the experience of my true self.

A: Wu Hsin cannot give you the experience of what you are while you continuously provide yourself with the experience of what you aren't.

What then remains?

Q: Must I destroy my sense of being a person in order to be liberated?

A: Yes and no.

You needn't burn down your hut to exit your hut. You can walk out the door.

Consciousness opens the door for the transcendence of consciousness. Until that occurs, consciousness experiences its manifestation via its instrument, the psychosomatic organism.

Q: Please tell me once again about my true essence, Master.

A: Nothing can appear unless there is something there to appear to, a locus of perception.

How can even void be known at all if there is no one to witness it?

One is neither the body nor the mind, yet aware of both. When the constant noise of the mental activity is stilled, peace reveals itself as ever-present.

Q: Beloved Wu Hsin, which practice is best for me to attain enlightenment?
A: What can an icicle do to return itself to water?
A human being is only an object, the instrument of experiencing. How could an object transform itself into that which is the essence? One is where one is because of everything one has done. One is where one is in spite of everything one has done.
As such, what one does or doesn't do loses its relevance.

Q: Master, there is so little time. Soon I will die. How can accelerate my becoming perfect?
A: At the time of death, what dies? Only the idea of being something in particular.
Becoming requires time whereas no time is required to be what you are. First see what you really are and then decide if becoming anything else is required.

Q: Master, is there an end to the discovery of what I really am?
A: No, because what you really are is infinite.
Q: My understanding no longer deepens. My frustration grows daily. What do you suggest for me?
A: Until the psychosomatic identification is released, understanding cannot go beyond the intellectual and intellectual understanding is not Understanding. You can use the intellect to know what you are not. Whatever you are, to know That, the intellect is of no use.
If you are stuck at this stage, surrender all to your god. In time, you will begin to feel that the god you've been surrendering to is none other than your own self.

Q: What must I do to reach heaven?
A: Were you an independent entity, there might be something for you to do. But you are not. All this talk is like believing that the reflection can improve the reflecting surface.
There is nothing for you to do. Allow that which brought you here to take you there.
Q: Where is the consciousness located?
A: When something is everywhere, where is it located?
As you don't need to know the location of your eyes in order to see, preoccupation with the location of consciousness is yet another distraction.

Q: Master, I come here to await your grace.
A: Why wait for something that has already arrived, for something that never leaves?

Q: Master Wu Hsin, I have been meditating for more than ten years yet I am still unhappy. Is my practice to be faulted?
A: Happiness is not determined by the feelings that are experienced. It is in the equanimity of standing apart from the feelings. Happiness is unmoved in the face of whatever negative feelings appear in the same way that the sun is unaffected by clouds.
It cannot be attained by any "one" and is self-shining in the presence of no "one". You can be happy in the world only when you are free of it.

Q: Master, my meditation is quite often fragmentary and frequently interrupted. What do you suggest for me?
A: Moving attention away from thoughts disempowers them and breaks their trance.
Q: Master, you are always completely unaffected by whatever happens. How do you do this? Can you teach it to me?
A: Black smoke may soil walls, but the sky is unaffected.
You are the sky. See it and be finished.

Q: Master Wu Hsin, I have been trying to monitor my progress. However, I really have no map, no way to understand if I am progressing. Do you have such a map?
A: The arrival of clear sight is sudden, like a frayed rope snapping. Whereas the fraying is gradual, the snapping happens in an unexpected instant.

Q: Master, what does it mean to know something directly?
A: Every thing known is known through some intermediary, the senses or the mind processes. Only being, I am, is known directly. Remain with yourself, don't get lost among objects.

Q: Master Wu Hsin, my self control is weak. How can I strengthen it?
A: The idea of self control is yet another egoic delusion. You can never control yourself as there is no second one to control the first.

The love affair with one's ideas must end. Emptied of all ideas, naked, one sees the Primordial Ground upon which all phenomena take its stand.

Q: Master, why do you not share with us your own experiences so that we can better come to know you?
A: They are unimportant. Know the truth of yourself and you will know Wu Hsin intimately.

Q: Master Wu Hsin, your teaching is most profound. However, are we not merely exchanging new concepts for old?
A: Any and all concepts are open to question. The only thing that cannot be questioned is existence, this clear sense that I am. Disregard all concepts, including those of Wu Hsin, and abide in what cannot be questioned.
Q: Master Wu Hsin, what is the difference between my reality and the reality of which you speak?
A: The only reality you have ever known is the reality of your beliefs.
However, when clear sight occurs, there appears a sudden void where you previously thought you were.

Q: Master, can you provide me with what I need?
A: What you need will come to you, if you are not preoccupied with what you don't need.

Q: Master, I have had great visions. What meaning should I assign to them?
A: What appears disappears.
You are that within which everything appears and disappears. This is their meaning, that they point back to what you are.

Q: Must my behavior be perfect in every moment of everyday?
A: To realize That which you are is not dependent on your proper behavior or correct conduct. It is not dependent on any condition: not on becoming and changing, not on some event in time.

Q: Master Wu Hsin, I want to be a better person. How may this be accomplished?

A: You have a role to play in the functioning of the world. Don't be concerned with it.
If the role needs improvement, adjustment or modification, leave it to the One Who assigned the role to take care of it.

Q: Master, I am feeling lost; can you provide me with direction?
A: Whether you are is not open to question. What you are is the direction of the investigation.

Q: Master, I have endless responsibilities and no time for looking within. What can I do?
A: Begin by re-examining your responsibilities. Let That which planted the trees provide them with the necessary water.
Q: Master, I wish to turn away from the world and retreat to the forests for my meditation. May I have your approval?
A: Retreating to the forest is not turning away from the world. It is merely changing your location in the world.
The ephemeral feeling of "I Amness" is the gateway to the Self. It is available in every moment, in every location, to those who are not otherwise distracted.

Q: Master, I am dissatisfied with my progress. My understanding does not deepen. Can you advise me?
A: There is no progress in what is real. What is there to progress to?
All notions of progress belong to the imagined world. It is like building a road to a town which doesn't exist.
Releasing them constitutes what you call progress.

Q: Master, how can you suggest that no practice is required? How can one progress without practice?
A: Regardless of the practice, when someone practices, it reinforces the notion of there being "someone". In the absence of practice, in the absence of any mental or physical movement, what are you?

Q: Master Wu Hsin, I have been told that you can help me become unlimited. If this is so, please instruct me in your ways.
A: First, find who it is who assigned limitation to you. You will find it is only yourself, as you have defined yourself. Limitation is the very essence of personality.

Investigate whether or not you have been lying to yourself. That is all.

Q: Master, my feelings of being something separate and apart are quite strong. I want to feel the essential unity but I don't. Am I doomed to this small existence?
A: Separation is the thought "I am this body and this mind". Relinquish this thought and then see if you remain separate.

Q: Master, why do I not see what you see?
A: You have accepted your mind as your teacher. You listen to it and obey its instructions. Little wonder you have gone so far from your true nature.

Q: Your reputation is known far and wide. May I humbly ask you, Master, why should I believe what you advise?
A: Wu Hsin does not ask you to believe.
Behave as if what I say is true and judge Wu Hsin by what actually ensues. Then, if belief is necessary, it will flower.

Q: Master Wu Hsin, this is the first time I am here with you. My life knows no happiness. Can you help me?
A: Wu Hsin helps no one.
If you give a bowl of rice to a starving man and he refuses to eat it, have you helped him? In eating the rice, he helps himself.
Here too, you help yourself when you take what has been given. Understanding this, are you ready to help yourself?

Q: Master, why don't more people come to be with you? Does the lack of attendance trouble you?
A: Those who are thirsty come to the water. The water doesn't worry about how many come or do not come.

Q: Master, what is meant by "apperception"?
A: Everyone is ensnared in a net of concepts. Tearing holes in the net is accomplished by eliminating concepts. The fewer the concepts, the larger the hole.
Apperception is understanding in the absence of concepts.

Q: Master, how do I remove this sense of "mine" which pervades so much?
A: When Wu Hsin has a brief stay in a guest house, he dare not claim the water pitcher beside the bed as "mine".
In much the same way, when one understands that this seeming life is merely a brief stay, the notion of "mine" will not arise.

Q: Can you show me that of which you teach?
A: Like the wind can only be seen by its effects, this force can be seen as thoughts, speech and actions.
It has no requirement for continuity. It is indestructible and untouchable.
Understand that only the false wants to insure that it goes on.

Q: Master, what is duality?
A: Duality is the mingling of I and not-I.

Q: Master, how am I to reach the Beyond?
A: Give up your fascination with your imaginary creations and then see if anything more is required.

Q: Master, I have listened to you give instruction to many others, each suitable to their dispositions. What is your instruction for me?
A: Return to that state prior to the arising of self consciousness.
Examine the view there and then see if anything else is required.

Q: Please look into my heart, Master Wu Hsin, and tell me what is yet to be seen clearly that holds me back.
A: You have not yet come far enough to understand that you are the subject of all phenomena.
You have yet to see that object-entity you have created to be yourself is yet another phenomenon to be known, but not the knower.

Q: Master, my understanding is that the goal is to abide as the seer. Is this correct?
A: When one looks at the triad of the seer, the seeing and the seen, one mistakes the seer for the subjectivity.
This is not so. The seer is the instrument of the subjectivity, which is the seeing.
It is in this Seeing that the triad is reduced to unity.

Q: Master, why do advise removing the attention from names and forms?
A: Finite bodies all come to an end, but that which possesses and uses the body, is infinite, without limit, eternal, indestructible.

Q: Master, how can a student recognize the Infinite?
A: It cannot be recognized because it cannot be cognized.
It cannot be remembered because it is never not now.

Q: Master, why is consciousness so important?
A: Just as light is required to see shadows, consciousness is required for the perception of the world.
The absence of one is the absence of both. Yet, even this is not final.
That which watches the stream of one's consciousness must be prior to said consciousness. What is that?

Q: Master Wu Hsin, I come before you because I am not seeing any results from my efforts. What do you advise me to do?
A: As sunlight hitting an object creates a shadow, the light of consciousness hitting the form of its instrument creates what in essence is also a shadow, the seeming self.
What efforts can such a shadow make?
Can you cook food on a painting of a fire?

Q: Master Wu Hsin, I have studied the ancient texts for many years and I feel that I understand them well. What is the need, therefore, to accept you as my teacher?
A: The study of sacred texts is of inferior quality to the realization of the truths the texts contain.
In the same way, the teacher is unimportant; only the teaching matters.
The teacher is merely the instrument through which the teaching manifests.

Q: Master, what happens to me after I die?
A: Why do you have this interest in what happens after death when you still retain such a poor understanding of what happens prior to death?
Why make death the reference point? All this is a distraction.

Death only has meaning in terms of the virtual entity who is caught up in the imagination of a solid, permanent self enduring for all time. Is this what you are?

Q: Master, can you clarify yet again what I am?
A: The body, with its personality, its identity, all its sentient functions, is an object.
That which knows the body, that which provides the sentience to the body, cannot be an object.
You are That.

Q: Master, what do you mean by "resting"?
A: All objects are pointers like the finger pointing at the raven in the tree.
Each points back to the Subject, in Whose absence, objects have no existence. To disregard the pointers, the objects, and to abide in the Subjective, is resting.

Q: Master, do those who follow your teachings reach heaven?
A: For those who understand Wu Hsin, all the world is heaven.

Q: Master Wu Hsin, I have a deep yearning to go to the Beyond. Will you take me there?
A: To speak of "beyond" is looking in the wrong direction.
Better is the continuous movement in the direction of "before". Find that line of demarcation where this "you" started and step over it.

Q: Master, if I hold fast to this consciousness, does the world disappear?
A: It disappears for some and not for others. In either case, the world becomes unimportant.

Q: Why is happiness so elusive?
A: People spend all their lives seeking happiness in one way or another, and the proof that they never obtain it is that they never stop seeking it.
It is now time to re-examine the validity of where the searching has been taking place.
Wu Hsin declares that this is not where happiness can be found.

Q: Master, the pains in my body make it difficult for me to put your teachings into practice. What do you advise?
A: The body is a borrowed thing; it must be returned. Turn the attention to what borrowed it.
Then, be still.

Q: My Master, the aches of my body and the incessant thoughts of my mind make it difficult for me to focus. What advice can you give me so that I can move into alignment?
A: The body and the mind work in accordance with their predispositions. Being neither, how are you affected?
Where is the need for alignment?

Q: Master Wu Hsin, could you speak more about the mind?
A: All the discussions about the mind are produced by the mind itself for its own continuation and expansion.
Remember that the conditioned mind can only provide conditioned responses.
Then you will not use it for this.

Q: Why has my god failed to help me?
A: Your god is not a thing; it is no thing.
If being nothing is good enough for your god, let it be good enough for you too.

Q: Master, please restate for me what is to be gained?
A: It is like believing that you have lost your pouch and then subsequently finding it. Nothing is gained because the pouch was always your own. In this sense, there is nothing to become.
All becoming is in service to the ego.

Q: Master Wu Hsin: I cannot meditate. My mind is filled with fears. How can I dispel them?
A: The idea of ownership creates fear. All "my's" need protection against loss.
As such, to live fearlessly is to live without "mine".
Q: How is peace to be attained?

A: There are two types of peace. The lesser is the absence of disturbance. The greater is that which is unassailable by disturbance. If you settle for the former, you have once again acquiesced to that which comes and goes.

You are the immaculate field of consciousness. Whatever appears in you cannot be you.

What you are is Peace Itself.

Q: Master, how can this small, limited person reach the Great Unity?
A: You define yourself as a name and a form and by the contents of your mind. You are not the body.

You are the conscious presence, the very Knowing of every thing. Of course you feel limited. When you identity with the particular, how can you not feel limited?

Accept my words and integrate them into your life. Then, all will reach fruition.

Q: Master Wu Hsin, my nature is dark. I cannot control it. What do you advise?
A: You are not your nature. This nature belongs to this body but you are neither.

The psychosomatic apparatus has a life of its own. Yet, it is not yours and you need not make it so.

All is because you are. Grasp this point firmly and deeply and dwell on it repeatedly.

Q: Dearest Master, please help me understand this idea of Conscious Being.
A: You are conscious of your individual existence and therefore must be something prior to it. This Being Consciousness is the original experience of differentiation from the Unmanifest.

From this, all else unfolds.

Q: Master Wu Hsin, so much is ephemeral. Please illuminate for me what is truly lasting that I may seek it out?
A: Anything lasting such as lasting peace or lasting happiness, can't be provided by anything temporary. Anything in time is temporary. Only "now" stands outside of time. Seek "now", it is the easiest to find.

Q: Master, you have shown me the way. Soon, I will have all that I desire. My eternal thanks I extend to you.
A: A word of caution. You now perceive a hole in your prison cell's wall big enough to jump through.
Be warned that what awaits on the other side of that wall, that which you are so keen to jump into, is the abyss.

Q: Why do you claim that the world and myself arise together?
A: In the absence of phenomena, "me" has nothing to hold, to cling to.
The non-dual is anathema to "me". Isn't it paradoxical that so many "me's" are trying to attain it?

Q: My Master, can you show me the absolute state of being?
A: The Absolute cannot be known directly.
Like the wind, it can only be known by its effects.

Q: I have been ill for quite some time. My body has numerous problems. How can I follow your teaching?
A: When you say "my body", who is this "my" distinct from the body?
If your neighbor has numerous problems, you are not affected. Treat your body as your neighbor.
Where, then, is any problem?

Q: My Master, what do you mean when you suggest that I "go back the way you came"?
A: The arrival of self consciousness is the movement away from the universal to the individual.
Going back the way you came means moving from the individual to the universal to the transcendent.

Q: Master Wu Hsin, when will I awaken?
A: You are like the man with a hen who wants to cut it in two, eating one half and keeping the other for laying eggs.
A person can never wake up whereas That Which Is is always awake.

Q: Why do you insist that no effort is necessary?
A: Why look for the sun with a candle?

One awakens spontaneously; one falls into sleep spontaneously. What occurs between these two also occurs spontaneously. There is no need for effort.
Can effort make you taller?

Q: Master, if one eliminates everything, then nothing remains. How does this activity lead to clear sight?
A: When everything is gone, what remains is that which certifies that everything is gone.
One might refer to this as the Sought.

Q: Master Wu Hsin, kindly guide my return to the Absolute. I ask for nothing more and nothing less.
A: One becomes an individual, so to speak, by thinking about that individual virtually every moment.
One returns to the Absolute in the same fashion.

Q: My Master Wu Hsin, I am confused. Should not waking up be my goal?
A: Whatever can wake up can go to sleep again.
To realize that which never slept is all that is required.

Q: My Master, how to discriminate between the good and the bad?
A: All such judgments originate in the mind and are structured relative to the individual.
Go behind the mind and you will find that good and bad don't exist.

Q: Master, what is the best method for studying your teaching?
A: What Wu Hsin teaches cannot be studied. It is only taught via listening. One allows it to sink in deeply and one ruminates over it. The seeds thus planted then yield their fruits.

Q: Is there a singular impediment to the attainment of clarity?
A: You know only what the senses inform. All experience is purely relative to them. Therefore, you never get past this relative to the Absolute.
The Pure Energy is not perceivable; only Its appearances, sound, heat, light etc. can be perceived.

Q: Master Wu Hsin, which is superior: matter or mind?

A: Matter is spacial whereas mind is temporal. This spacio-temporal field is the screen on which the world appears.
It is known by the Light of Consciousness.

Q: Master Wu Hsin, my teacher advised me to repeat "I am All" continuously but its promise has not been realized. My question is whether or not I should cease this practice?
A: Even a parrot can be taught to say "I am All".
Ultimately, the highest practice, so to speak, is to be free of practices. Begin by getting rid of everything, all previous acquisitions relating to mind and body.
Once this is accomplished, one gets rid of the practice itself and one is then free from all practices. This is the practice; continue it until it leaves you.

Q: Master, what assurances do I have that I can exist without this body?
A: Look and see. You do so every night in sleep. You have no knowledge of this body in sleep. Yet, you know you slept.
What is this Knowing?

Q: Master Wu Hsin: This is my first time in the Hall in your presence. What do you teach?
A: Wu Hsin teaches a single trick: how to be in the water without getting wet.

Q: Master Wu Hsin, what practice do you recommend for me?
A: All practices sustain what one is not. What one is requires no practice to be. Let Being be your practice.

Q: My Master, I have been with you for more than fifteen years. Yet, I remain incomplete. What is my failing?
A: For so long as you continue to avoid the means while insisting on its ends, this seeming failure will continue.
Wu Hsin shall reiterate: The only path to follow is the path by which you came. Retrace your steps assiduously and you will see.

Q: Master, my thoughts make it impossible for me to remain quiet. I feel powerless. What do you advise?

A: Your hear the beautiful song of the sparrow. It appears inside your head. Yet, you don't claim the song to be yours. Why is it that you claim that the thought that seems to appear inside your head is yours?

It is not; it is mere appearance, like a cloud in the sky. It need not receive your attention.

Q: I come here today to challenge you, Wu Hsin. What you teach is a soulless view of the world. Can you deny this?

A: Quite the contrary, Wu Hsin affirms this.

Wu Hsin does not deal in fictions, in stories crafted on hearsay or in the absence of evidence.

If you have proof of the existence of a soul, I return your challenge: produce it now.

Q: My Great Master, how can this one be worthy of you?

A: To be worthy of me is to not be separate from me. This is achieved by the death of individuality.

Q: Master Wu Hsin, I am 101 years of age. Soon, I will be finished, yet the goal has not been reached. With so little time remaining for me, what do you advise?

A: It is only your body that is short of time, not you. You are not bound. When you truly understand yourself, you realize eternity.

Q: Master, how does enlightenment come about?

A: The subjective Conscious Life Energy becomes entangled with its objective instrument. This entanglement must be undone, yet cannot be done by any individual.

Such disentanglement is deemed enlightenment.

Q: Master, it amazes me that you are always so even, never fazed by what occurs around you. How do you do this?

A: When everyone vacates this Hall, how is the Hall affected?

Clouds appear in the sky while the sun remains unfazed.

Q: Master, where is this Conscious Life Energy located inside me?

A: When speaking of something that is everywhere, the words "inside" and "outside" are meaningless.

Q: Master Wu Hsin, what is your advice for attaining the highest state?
A: As a man cannot claim to be destitute before examining the contents of his coin box, so you cannot claim to know what you do before you know what you are.
Therefore, the advice is to separate yourself from what you are not. What could be easier?

Q: Am I not the perceiver of everything?
A: The quality I-am perceives. This perceiving via the senses is a process whereas thinking about what was perceived creates a perceiver.

Q: Master, I don't understand how you can say that I am not real. Can you help me to see this?
A: An "I" is an unexamined assumption. How can you be a person when you are that which observes the person?

Q: Oh, Master, where do I begin?
A: Beginning points are numerous. Recognize that you are never reaching a point where you remain fulfilled.
Discover that you do not really know what you want in life beyond the survival essentials.
See that the mind is not interested in peace but only in its own pursuits.
I believe that these will keep you occupied.

Q: Must I not examine the teacher before I put myself entirely into his hands?
M: By all means examine. But what can you learn?
Only as he appears to you from your viewpoint, from your established standard.
How many times has it been explained that Wu Hsin is not a person? What does examination of such a person satisfy?

Q: Master, how do you describe this unity?
A: It is one continuous whole over which the three states of waking, dream and sleep pass.

Once this is apperceived, one has returned from never having been away.

Q: Master, all my searching has failed. Does this mean that I am not worthy?
A: Not at all; you are most worthy. The only problem is that you have been ill-advised.
Where can you search for that which is non-objective?

Q: There are those who advise we must go beyond the world. What say you, Master Wu Hsin?
A: Would it not seem reasonable that prior to going beyond the world, one have full understanding of that state before the world? Attain that and then see if anything more is required.

Q: Master Wu Hsin, once I acquire clarity of sight, will I view others differently?
A: Yes, without Knowledge, one cannot know the other. With Knowledge, one is the other.
Q: Master, my happiness comes and goes. What can I do to give it stability?
A: One cannot speak of "my happiness" as if it were an exclusive possession. One cannot use "my happiness" as one would use "my wife".
The happiness that Wu Hsin speaks of is universal; it cannot come and go. It is inherent in you, in your innermost being.

Q: Which path is best for me?
A: By whatever path you go, you will have to lose yourself in it.
Self realization is only the realization of that which is not true.
Whatever approach aligns with your disposition is the path to pursue.
The notion of paths is as useless as back pockets on a shirt.
There are no paths to what you already are.

Q: Master, does destiny control my course in life?
A: The tree is latent in the seed. It is already there.
This is so for all seeds and their fruits.

Q: Master, what is reality?

A: Reality is thoughtlessness. When one is without thought, one's vision is clear and reality is discerned.

Q: Master Wu Hsin, I have been your faithful student for many years now. However, the goal continues to elude me. What is my failing?
A: You indeed sense that you may not be what you believe yourself to be. But, you refuse to investigate it with sufficient depth for fear of losing what you have.
You are not yet willing to relinquish your sense of continuity.
Wu Hsin advises there is nothing to fear.

Q: Master, why do you refuse to recommend any practice?
A: All practices require doing something. As such, they reinforce the cage that holds you, the notion of a doer.
Any method, no matter how promising, fortifies the structure of the ego, further increasing the chaos. It is like tasking a cat to guard a bowl of milk.
Only being requires no doing. This is the one true practice.

Q: Master Wu Hsin, kindly direct me back to the source of all things.
A: To know the world, you remove attention from its support.
To know the support, you remove attention from the world.
Q: Master, I yearn for nothing less than the infinite. Can you give it to me?
A: A price must be paid for the infinite. That price is everything finite.
Are you willing to pay it?

Q: You have stated that beingness is the key to your teaching. Why is that?
A: The sense "I am" exists in all three states. When it identifies with a body, "I am" becomes self consciousness.
That which knows "I am" is what should be made the focus of attention.

Q: Where does this consciousness come from, Master?
A: Asking where consciousness comes from is like asking when time began.

Q: Master, I continue to be confused whether the world is real or not.

A: Let the world bother about its reality or falsehood. Find out first about your own reality. Then all things will become clear.

Q: Master, I have forgotten my true nature. What am I?
A: One's true nature need not be remembered nor can it ever be forgotten because it is ever-present.
The changeless Self never changes. Therefore, anything that changes cannot be what you are.
Do not preoccupy yourself with "What am I?" Defining yourself will not help you; delineating what you are not is sufficient.

Q: Master Wu Hsin, I have been sitting and watching my mind. Is this the correct approach?
A: The correct approach is to clarify who is watching the mind. Is the mind watching the mind or is it something else? If it is something other than mind watching the mind, then observe this watcher.

Q: Master Wu Hsin, I have sat at your feet for many years now, yet still I have not attained. Where is the flaw in my practice?
A: No source of illumination is required in order to see the sun. One simply turns toward it and rests the attention on it.
How can you expect to see the sun if your attention is fixated elsewhere?

Q: Master, what needs to be given up in order to realize the state of Wu Hsin?
A: Only thought.
You can't consume pure water from a dirty cup.

Q: Master, can you give some direction so that I may find peace?
A: Any direction will take you away from where you are. This peace you seek is where you are.
Merely stop masking it with thought. You know that you are. Without this, you cannot know the world.
Discern by what it is that you know that you are and stay there.

Q: Master Wu Hsin, your wisdom is indeed infinite. Can you describe for me what it is that you have gotten?

A: I got what I need to have. I see what I need to see and I know what I need to know. I am no longer distracted.

Q: Master, would a vow of silence be helpful to me?
A: Such a vow merely restrains the speaker, yet does nothing to quiet the source of the words.
Before any word is spoken, it is in mind. True silence is silence of mind.

Q: Master, I have yet to attain the Ultimate. What is the impediment?
A: Clinging to the idea that only what has a name and a shape exists, the Ultimate cannot be available to you. As such, searching within the phenomenal is searching in the wrong place.

Q: Master Wu Hsin, can you teach me about the witness, the one who watches?
A: When there are phenomena to be witnessed, the witness appears. In the absence of phenomena, the witness exists in potential, as does the totality of manifestation. In truth, there is no witness, only witnessing as function.
Therefore, we can say that the witnessing and manifestation rise and set together.

Q: Master, what must I do to move beyond the world?
A: Is the world within you or outside of you? Does it exist apart from you?
See through the world to your own being. In so doing, the drive to move beyond the world falls away.

Q: Master Wu Hsin, I humbly beg you to free me from this bondage.
A: Believing in hearsay or in thoughts that are incorrect leads one to incorrect conclusions.
If there is any freeing to be done at all, one might say it is only to be freed from the idea of one who is bound.
Those who look deeply discern that they have never been bound and therefore have no need to be freed.

Q: My Master, when I look around me, all that I see is unhappiness interrupted by brief periods of happiness. How can this be resolved?
A: Happiness and unhappiness are two sides of the same coin.

What remains when the coin is thrown away?

Q: Master, I have been striving for so long. What must be done to bring an end to it?
A: All striving is toward becoming.
When the notion of becoming falls away, striving falls away.
To be is effortless; only being something in particular requires effort.

Q: Master, what you speak of is so beautiful. Unfortunately, to me it is lost. What must I do?
A: You must simply change the way you look at things.
What is ever-present can never be lost. It only seems lost to you because you are otherwise engaged.

Q: Master, how can you assert that I am eternal?
A: Did you not exist prior to this birth, dormant in the seed of your father in the same way that the sunflower lies dormant in the sunflower seed? And was your father not dormant in the seed of his father? This regression leads back to the so-called beginning.
As such, you have always been, in potential, awaiting the right time and place for your arrival.

Q: Master, all the practices I have done in the past have failed to provide the desired results. What would you suggest for me?
A: Be as you are and stop being as you aren't. What course, what practice, needs to be undertaken for you to be as you are?
What one appears to be is framed by one's ideas and beliefs. Setting all of these aside is the return to one's naturalness.

Q: Master, you teach that the way things actually are has been obscured. This confuses me. Can you expand on this?
A: Rice has poured over your precious jade. How, then, to see the jade? Simply remove the rice.
What is this rice that Wu Hsin alludes to? It is thought.

Q: Why do you say that being knowledgeable is an impediment?
A: You consider yourself knowledgeable because you know worldly things like the rising and setting of the sun.
Do you think the sun has any interest in when it rises and sets?

The mind is easily distracted with irrelevancies. Until you can discriminate between the important and the unimportant, you will remain lost regardless of Wu Hsin's words.

Q: Master, how can I find peace?
A: Peace is easy to find.
In total stillness, that is, both mental and physical stillness, all there is is peace.

Q: Master Wu Hsin, can you help me understand my god?
A: Asking "why did my god do this?" is like asking why the sun grows the grass. You may come to understand the "how" of it, but never the "why".
Q: Master, what is the relationship between mind and identity?
A: The mind is the set of processes leading us to think that we think. The identity that is commonly referred to is a temporary one. It is always in flux and is little more than the sum of everything you call "mine".

Q: Master, my life is tossed about by numerous problems. How can one such as I get clear of all this?
A: Thought is an epiphenomenon of the life energy. The sum of thoughts, mind, is the creator of the pseudo-subject and all of its objects, including the body.
Stillness is the antidote to mind. In it, not a single problem can be found.

Q: Master, how can I stay present?
A: Presence is always present. This may sound trivial, but it is in fact pivotal. Presence cannot be lost so all notions of searching for it or attaching to it are only delusion.

Q: Master, can you describe the path to Reality?
A: There are no paths to Reality whereas the paths to unreality are numerous.
If one abides at the source of one's being, what path need be prescribed? All paths are movements away from this abidance.

Q: Master Wu Hsin, can it be said that the Source is my center? Is it your instruction that I abide in this center?

A: To speak of one's center is to give credence to individuality. This Source is both the center and the circumference. If you like, call it the center of infinity.

Q: Master, why is it that so many go away without receiving your help?

A: Those who are unwilling to examine every belief they hold cannot expect to benefit from being seated with Wu Hsin.

Q: Master Wu Hsin, I am a simple man. Can you give me a simple practice that will allow one such as I to succeed?

A: Those insistent on a practice need do nothing more than continuously reject the false.

Q: Master, am I to be totally alone and unsupported in this quest?

A: Not at all. That which you are accompanies you to the goal because It is the goal.

Q: Master, what is the highest state?

A: The highest state is not a state because all states are bound to time. That which was prior to time is the highest.

Q: Master Wu Hsin, you advise us to discern the real from the unreal. How to do this?

A: Don't confuse what is real with what appears. What appears, disappears.

You can't say that it was real "for a while". That which sees is present at the time of the appearance and at the time of the disappearance.

What is real is always. That is the measuring stick.

In that sense, all experience is temporary except for That which is experienced without the senses and without thought.

This is the direct knowledge of I.

Q: Master, you have spoken of a deeper knowing. Can you say more about this?

A: In the absence of a reflecting surface, how do you know that you have eyes?

You know because there is an inherent Knowing in operation at all times.

When the attention is turned toward this Knowing and remains there, the allure of the world dissipates.

Q: Master, how long will it be before I have reached your understanding?
A: For some, it is instantaneous. They hear the words and in a flash it is done.
For others, it is like wind and water wearing away rock.

Q: Master, where is this Conscious Life Energy?
A: Where is it not?

Q: Master Wu Hsin, I am afraid to stop all thinking. The nothingness that would remain scares me.
A: Absence of thoughts does not mean a void because what remains is the knower of the void.
This is what you are and what must be discovered.

Q: Is the recognition of the Conscious Life Energy the ultimate or is there further to go?
A: First stabilize there and then see if the question arises.

Q: Master, the world I see when I wake up is the same world I saw before I slept. It is a constant; is this not so?
A: That which is in perpetual flux can never be said to be the same. One cannot bathe in the same river on successive days. One can say that it seems the same, but it is not so.

Q: Master, my consciousness requires purification. What do you advise for me?
A: "My consciousness"? How do you claim to own it?
When you go to the river and fill a pail with water, dare you call the water in the pail "mine"?

Q: Master, do you continue to think?
A: There are thoughts. However, my thinking, like my digestion, is unconscious.

Q: Master, what is the proper way to conduct myself?
A: Codes of conduct pertain to individuals. Wu Hsin does not speak of or to individuals.

Q: Master, my yearning to reach the end of my search continues. I have traversed many roads, yet I still have not arrived. Am I destined to fail?

A: All needs, wants, hopes, wishes, ambitions, pleasures or dissatisfactions are creations of an individual. Only humans experience these.

All searching is a search for completeness, to find what must be added from "out there".

Once it is discerned that one is already complete, searching naturally, of itself, falls away.

Q: Master, I have experienced periods of great peace and tranquility. Then, the world reasserts its hold on me and the peace is lost. What can I do to hold this state of peace that I have had?

A: If one's inner state is dependent upon outer events, it is false and must pass.

All outward movement is movement away from inherent peace. When the energy of attention is removed from the world, the world will lose its hold on you.

Q: Master, I see the world, but I don't understand it. Can you help me to see it more clearly?"

A: It's all about viewpoint, about the center of reference.

From our view, the sun rises and sets.

But to speak of rising and setting from the vantage point of the sun is a meaningless statement.

We say that the moon shines in the same way as we say that there is a person that acts.

Yet, it is not that the moon is shining.

Rather, it is merely reflecting the light of the sun.

Persons, too, are only the reflected light of That which shines on them and provides their support.

Like the tartness in a lime or the sweetness of honey, the person is merely the quality or expression of the organism.

Q: Master Wu Hsin, how can I overcome my fear of death?

A: No one is born, no one dies.

There is merely the beginning, the duration and the end of an event, an objectified life in space and time.

When you become clear that you are not this body, but that it is your instrument, then worries about death dissolve.
In essence, death dies.

Q: Master Wu Hsin, if I follow what you advise to its conclusion, what will happen to me?
A: What happens to salt when it is thrown into water?

Q: Master, I am possessed by fear. What can I do?
A: What is fear? Fear is "other".
As long as one considers oneself to an object in a world of objects, fear will remain a component of experience.
When the eyes are opened to a new way of seeing, the result is a new way of being.
Q: My Master, how may I repay you for this gift?
A: Be what you are. Remain as what you are. This is the greatest repayment to Wu Hsin and to the world.

Q: Master Wu Hsin, what is the need for listening to your discourse?
A: Before a pail can be filled with water, the cracks and holes must be repaired. Otherwise, nothing is held.
Consider the words of Wu Hsin to be sealant.

Q: Master, I will give up all of my possessions if that is what is required. Is it so?
A: No possessions need be given up. All that is to be relinquished is the notion of "mine".

Q: What is realization, Master?
A: Suddenly, you realize that what you considered normal was not really normal. Said realization is an instantaneous shift from an individual existence to existence as it is. There is no longer a willingness to exchanging peace for thought. What had been considered to be the mind is transformed into That to which 'I' refers.

Q: Master, can you please explain what you mean by knowingness?
A: This knowingness did not appear because you submitted a requisition for it. It arose spontaneously. It is that which reports on the three states of sleep, dream, and waking.

Q: Master, is this higher state that you speak of something that comes and goes?
A: To that which is everywhere, coming and going has no meaning.

Q: Master Wu Hsin, do you advise that I renounce everything?
A: No, you need only renounce your attachment to everything.
Q: Master, how can a limited being realize the Unlimited?
A: You have become so acclimated to limitation that, for many, the idea of limitlessness is unfathomable.
The regression is from "I am an individual" to "I am the Totality" to "I am No thing".
That which is nameless, formless, and attributeless cannot be described. The only means to it is the rejection of all that is not-That.

Q: Master Wu Hsin, for over twenty years I have been seeking liberation. All my efforts have ended in failure. What do you advise?
A: Talk of the liberation of any phenomenon is foolishness.
Until you are willing to loosen your grip on your identification with the body and the mind, any effort will continue to end in failure.

Q: Master, I am considering taking a vow of silence. What is your opinion?
A: Unless you are able to keep the mind silent, such a vow will have no value.

Q: Master, how can I attain union with the ultimate?
A: To seek union presupposes separation.
There is no need to seek union; simply verify that there is, in fact, separation.

Q: Master, your words are subtle, yet complex. Where can I begin?
A: Begin with complete surrender to the words of Wu Hsin.
Do that first, await the results, and then see if there need be anything more to do.

Q: Master, kindly detail for me the efforts you require I make in order to be free.
A: All effort is rooted in the body-sense. To one who does not identify with a body, what effort can be made?

Q: Master, I decided to raise my hand before I raised my hand. How is this point of view flawed?
A: It is flawed in that it is incomplete.
Before you decided to raise your hand, I decided to raise our hand.
This "I" is not this body that you see before you.
This "I" is that which you don't see before you but is what you find already present when you arise from sleep.

Q: Master, please tell me more about the Absolute.
A: Other than to declare it the potentiality, the mind cannot consider the Absolute.
Therefore, all words amongst us begin from the point of manifestation, that is, Consciousness and the phenomena that appear in it.

Q: Master, what you are asking us to do needs peace and quiet. I have neither. What am I to do?
A: Whereas the body has needs, the individual has wants. There is neither want nor need for peace and quiet; once the obstructions are removed, you will discern that you are peace and quiet itself.

Q: Master, what is the need for awakening?
A: There is none.
Only sleeping requires awakening. That which never sleeps does not.

Q: Master Wu Hsin, what must be done to transcend this body and this mind?
A: Only see that the body and the mind happen to you, but that you are neither.

Q: Master, the world creates so many obstacles for me. What am I to do?
A: The obstacles are not in the world, but are in your mind.
The principal activity of the brain is to represent the world that is external to it. The principal activity of the mind is to protect the body.
All sense perceptions are filtered through the mind before they become experience.
In the pure mind of the infant, no interpretation occurs.

Whatever comes and goes is a mental creation only, an appearance, like the blue of the sky or the blue in the ocean. When one abides behind the mental, all that is permanent shines.

Q: I can see that the whole world is only a dream. Yet, somehow, my troubles persist.
A: You might see the whole world as a dream, but until you understand that the dreamer is integral to the dream and not apart from it, your troubles will continue.

Q: Master, can you describe this Conscious Life Energy to which you refer?
A: It is That out of which the self consciousness arises and into which it will ultimately dissolve.
At the latest, this dissolution occurs at death. Yet, it can occur before.

Q: Master, how many more years until my personal awakening?
A: There are no personal awakenings; there are only awakenings from the personal.

Q: Master Wu Hsin, how much time is required for all this?
A: You have always been what you truly are, and always will be. In this regard, no time is required.

Q: Master, I come before you with great humility and ask this question: is a teacher necessary?
A: What is required is unlearning. Is a teacher necessary for that?

Q: There are those who argue that all we need to do is to develop virtue in ourselves. What say you, Master Wu Hsin?
A: Is this "you" anything more than the mind, the body, and the memory of a stream of events in which this "you" played its role?
By contrast, the real you is that onto which all those appeared.
All the virtue in the world cannot help you to discern this.

Q: Master, what is renunciation?
A: To renounce is to recognize and discard all that is not necessary.

Q: Master Wu Hsin, what is your instruction?

A: What do you have to do to be what you already are?
The only instruction is to stop being what you are not and to give up all ideas of personal attainment.
Q: Master, once I have your wisdom and insight, will all my problems be solved?
A: You repeatedly cycle through three aspects of life, namely, the waking, the dream and the sleep states. The so-called problems of one do not carry into any other whereas you are present in all.
How real, then, can they be?

Q: Master, what is the purpose of realization and what must I do to attain it?
A: You already know its purpose, the alteration of the unsatisfactory state that brought you here in search of realization.
Doing? What doing? Who is doing anything? What does a flower do to smell fragrant? What must a lake do to reflect the moon?

Q: Master Wu Hsin, what am I?
A: What is prior to the first thought "I am" is what you are.
Everything comes and goes in It. Even consciousness, the birthplace of duality, calls it father.
Its expressions may be infinite, yet It unifies them all.

Q: Why is your body sometimes ill and frail?
A: Because you believe you have a body, Wu Hsin appears to you as having a body. You may revisit this question if you so choose once your body identification is gone.

Q: Master, why do you tell us that life is only a dream?
A: It must be only a dream because it is a story you have imagined about yourself as the acting protagonist. It is an object dreaming that it had subjectivity.

Q: What can you give to me, Wu Hsin?
A: What can you take and what can you offer in return? You ask for everything, yet offer little. If you want to bargain, let us at least make it a fair one.

Q: Master, when I die, what dies?

A: The owner dies. The owner of the cart, the house and garden, the family, the body and its feelings, the mind, the experiences, the owner of the personal narrative.
That is what dies.

Q: How long must I wait for the event of enlightenment to come to me?
A: There is no need to await an event to confirm what you already are.
The only enlightenment there is is the cessation of confusion and imagination.

Q: Master Wu Hsin, I have gone to many masters yet none have been able to solve my problems. Can you?
A: The problems belong to the individual with a body. Virtually all the problems are the body's problems. You are neither an individual nor its problems.
See this and your problems are solved.

Q: Master, is there such a thing as a natural state? If there is, what is it?
A: The natural state is the state you revert to when your attention is not directed outward.

Q: Master, it seems to me that I am nearer to myself when I am awake than when I am dreaming. Is this not so?
A: Distance cannot be used for reference here. What you are you are always. What you appear to be may seem near or far.

Q: Master, why doesn't everyone come to sit with you?
A: Those that are not hungry don't go in search of vegetables.

Q: It is very difficult to give up this attraction to the bodily identity.
A: Indeed; as the attention moves away from the center, away from consciousness itself and toward the world, a distorting process is initiated. After several years, a reflected self arises in the infant and there is identification with it.
Wu Hsin declares that there is diversity in the world and a unity runs through the diversity. Where is the diversity when you are asleep? Identify with the unity and let the world see to itself.

Q: Master, what is the practice for achieving the natural state?
A: Cease imagining; cease fixating the attention on whatever appears.

Q: What steps do you prescribe for one such as myself?
A: How many steps must you take to reach yourself?
Investigate how it is that consciousness of the world and consciousness of the body rise and set together. This points to the correct address.

Q: Master Wu Hsin, thoughts interrupt my meditation unceasingly. What can I do to stop thinking?
A: You may hear your neighbors arguing. What difference does it make to you if you are disinterested?
Thoughts arise in endless succession. What difference does it make to you if you are disinterested?

Q: Master Wu Hsin, I have become lost in the whirlwind of my ideas. There is so much to consider. How do I sort through all this?
A: When you become entwined in the branches and leaves of the tree, you never get to the root. Without accessing the root, the seed is inaccessible.
What one sees keeps changing, but the Seeing remains fixed.
When the Seeing is gone, the world too is gone.
The end of Seeing is the return to the en potentia state. This Potential is unknowable.
Only the actual can be known.

Q: Master, What is holding me back?
A: When you refuse to open your eyes, what can you expect to see?
Clarity requires one to stop imagining.
Q: Master, must this work be so arduous?
A: No, it need not. What it makes it arduous is that you insist on dragging all your "there and then" into the here and now.

Q: Thank you, thank you, my beloved Master Wu Hsin for everything you have given me.
A: There is no need to thank Wu Hsin.

If you have a kilo of gold buried below your house, until you know it is there you appear to be poor.
Has the one who told you of its location made you wealthy?

Q: Master, what is the difference between us?
A: Relatively speaking, the difference is that your frame of reference is on what is lacking while mine is on the fullness of all things. From an absolute viewpoint, there are no differences.

Q: Master Wu Hsin, there are moments when I can see my god. Is this the highest?
A: In order to see your god, something had to be there to see; not a seer, but seeing. That is the highest and you are That.

Q: Master, what is gained from clarity?
A: Clarity is not a gain. It is a loss; a loss of seeking and searching, a loss of individuality, a loss of all acquisitions.

Q: Master Wu Hsin, where should I begin?
A: Beginning by questioning that which is habitual, that which is mechanical, in you.

Q: Master, I have been with you for many years, listened to every answer you have given to every question. Still, I feel no closer to my goal. What can I do now?
A: You need a hook to hang your concepts on, but Wu Hsin refuses to provide any. You expect that Wu Hsin's answers to your questions will create a mystical opening with clarity ensuing. Stop this foolishness.
Whatever concepts arise, see that you are none of them. The hopes you hang on Wu Hsin's answers then wither.

Q: Master, is there a most direct method to understand your teachings?
A: The direct method is to listen to the words of Wu Hsin and apply them to your life with total conviction. If you comply, you will cease pretending that what isn't, is superior to what is.

This will conclude the questioning.

Wu Hsin then offered the following instruction to the assembled:

It is only by theatre of the mind and its transient displays that the world shines.

Thus, the Knower of the mind holds true knowledge of the world.

The screen does not see what appears on it.

Images appear in the mind; what sees them?

One is aware of words spoken seemingly inside one's head; what hears them?

In other words, "What knows the mind?"

Now that you have heard, go …………….. and live accordingly.

Made in the USA
Lexington, KY
07 January 2015